Bill Lavender

city of god

POEMS

based on a distracted* reading of a dubious translation** of

DE CIVITATE DEI CONTRA PAGANOS

commonly known in English as

City of God

by

Saint Augustine of Hippo

*by life and media in the USA, beginning January 6, 2021, the day of the Trump insurrection, ending January 6, 2025, the day of his election certification.
**Marcus Dods editor/translator, 1872 edition, Gutenberg Ebook #45304.

MADHAT PRESS
CHESHIRE, MASSACHUSETTS
MMXXVI

city of god
by Bill Lavender
Copyright© 2026 by Bill Lavender, all rights reserved.

ISBN 978-1-968422-02-8 (pbk.)
Library of Congress Control Number: 2025943728

Publisher's Cataloging-in-Publication Data
Names: Lavender, Bill, 1951- .
Title: city of god / Bill Lavender.
Description: Cheshire, MA : MadHat, 2026. | Includes glossary. | Summary: Poems based on a distracted (by life, media, and politics in the USA) reading of a dubious translation (Marcus Dods editor/translator, 1872 edition) of the De civitate Dei, commonly known in English as City of God, by Saint Augustine of Hippo.
Identifiers: LCCN 2025943728 | ISBN 9781968422028 (pbk.)
Subjects: LCSH: Augustine, of Hippo, Saint, 354-430. De civitate Dei. | Poetry, Modern – 21st century. | History – Poetry. | Political science – Poetry. | Religion – Poetry. | LCGFT: Poetry. | BISAC: POETRY / Subjects & Themes / Political & Protest. | POETRY / American / General. | POETRY / Subjects & Themes / Religious.
Classification: LCC PS3612.A944 C58 2025 | DDC 811--dc23
LC record available at https://lccn.loc.gov/2025943728

MadHat Press
MadHat Incorporated
PO Box 422, Cheshire, MA 01225
www.madhat-press.com

Praise for *city of god*

Bill Lavender describes the origins of his riveting long poem, *city of god* (*pace* St. Augustine), as a "spiritual exercise," begun on the day of the insurrection in distracted dialogue with Augustine's original (albeit in "dubious translation," as Lavender ironically notes). Neither moralizing nor polemical, as was Augustine, Lavender sees our tarnished world with equilibrium, and even (quoting Augustine's *Homilies on the First Epistle of John*) love—not only for the beloved "face across / the table," but also for this "city of souls / ruled solely by / the lust to rule." By turns incisive cultural critique and erudite lyric meditation, Lavender's *city of god* is a stunning poetic record—of our times, and for the ages. This is a masterpiece!

—**Cynthia Hogue**, author of *instead, it is dark*

Few were as freaked out as I was when Bill Lavender revealed the colossal scope of the project he was working on. I (many of us!) feared hellish barriers to its publication. For four straight years, Bill had been thrilling us by reading sections—live, in New Orleans. And now, here's 326 pages of poems that virtuosically track the seismic political changes roiling below our feet. Here's Lavender straight up calling it: Christian Nationalism, and its downriver cultural debris. *city of god* stands as one of the richest, most experimental and authentic chronicles of our time.

—**Rodrigo Toscano**, author of *WHITMAN.CANNONBALL.PUEBLA.*

Bill Lavender responds to Augustine with this sprawling city of poems. The beautiful complexity of this book follows on the terrible chaos of January 6, 2021, the day he began writing responses to Augustine's calls., and ends with Trump's return to power. There's a world of learning here, but I keep coming back to the homeless woman who greets the poet at his car many mornings. She has one arm; in her remaining hand she holds an unlit cigarette. She talks about Jesus. She has children, but she's a virgin. Her name changes. She prays for Bill. Her city, which is also his, is New Orleans. Beautiful and corrupt, it contains the poet's multitudes. Lavender writes with rage and empathy into his own, and his nation's, last days.

—**Susan M. Schultz**, author of *I and Eucalyptus*

As one who teaches Augustine and has had his own long agon with him, I have endless admiration for Lavender's engagement with the ancient Berber. This book challenges the Saint's intellect, language, heart and moral spirit—and even yaks back at him through the lives and words of current city-dwellers (meet the one-armed New Orleans woman). Erudite, jazzy, perhaps sinful, this is the modern polis's earnest riposte to the creator of "original sin."

—**Peter Thompson**, translator of Fernando Arrabal's *Letter to General Franco*

Augustine's *City of God* is a thousand pages of passionate rhetoric to refute the pagan opinion that the Christians were to blame for the fall of Rome. Along the way Augustine reviews the Bible from beginning to end, explaining that this corrupt world has been from the start destined for eternity. Bill Lavender is not so sure. His *city of god* plays against Augustine's text, section by section (going back and forth between the Cities is a trip!), but in place of a pontificating saint we have a plain-speaking New Orleans poet reflecting, soberly and gorgeously, in his latter years, on a world again at the brink. Where Augustine is brash and polemic, Lavender is elegiac and compassionate. This is a truly astonishing work, one you'll want to live with for a while.

—**Norman Fischer,** author of *There was a clattering as...*

"i'll try not to drop my lyre on your head," the poet promises, but "i'm dreaming your dreams for you." A book of poetry—and a sharply-observed political and cultural critique— Bill Lavender's brilliant "reading through" of *City of God* is an invitation to Augustine's city to drape itself (like ghostly Spanish moss) over contemporary America. Responding to and updating the classic, Lavender offers readers the chance to drift or follow his *dérive* through "the city...neither future nor past" where dream and reality, past and present, weave in and out of each other as they do in the mind, imagination shaping the real and the real compelling imagination:

> here the west is reborn
> psychic pantheon
> stood down by casuistry
> and the 'right' of *jus imperium*
>
> bare desert imagining
> itself garden
> out of which, delirious,
> trump wandered

A wonderful antidote to the delirium of our epoch, Lavender's book offers a model of how to stay alive, present, and creative under pressure.

—**Laura Mullen,** author of *EtC*, translator of Stéphanie Chaillou's *something happens*

If you read one book opposing the Trump zeitgeist, read Bill Lavender's *city of god*. In poems that are multi-vocal and multi-focused, he toggles cities and ages and weaves prayers and curses for 1461 days. His masters are Dante and Dave Chappelle. No one has ever blended rage and empathy more eloquently.

—**Rodney Jones,** author of *Salvation Blues* and *Alabama*

Magnificently palimpsested through St. Augustine, counterpointed by exquisite self-reflexivity, Bill Lavender's 2025 monumental epic, *city of god*, highlights how Rome's fall, due to its own moral corruption and internal decay, resembles our current "city of romance," "a sacked city," "of law," "fable," "coded whispers" and "wailing blindnesses," bitcoin, TikTok, Zuckerburg, Alexa, police, politicians and suitcases of corporate cash. Punctuated by battlegrounds of urban warfare, sacraments, slaughters, scaffolds, desecration and decay—as we worship in a "forum of fakery," between fighting factions, fictions, frictions and predilections, Lavender's stunningly prescient august[inian] translation, underscores how history, "slurred through centuries," is cyclic; spiraling through a contemporaneous socio-political religiously solicitous cesspool festering in monstrous hysteria and hope. A dexterously textural, poignantly pivotal, "hurricane of passions."

—**Adeena Karasick**, author of *Ærotomania: The Book of Lumenations*

It amuses me (seriously) to think that Saint Augustine, upon receiving an advance copy of Bill Lavender's *city of god*, would have gone all out to learn English. Although the philosopher never mastered Greek, he would surely have thumbed his English-Latin lexicon from dawn to dusk to make sure he had fully grasped the countless fine details and all the satirical import of this teeming, scathing, mocking, rambunctiously salacious long-poem. Book-length, no, *tome*-length, this vigorous poetic sequence, which consists of a mesmerizing flow of both critical annotations and personal reflections "based on a distracted reading of a dubious translation..." is indeed the transcription of a *disputatio*, "augustine vs. lavender," as the poet himself points out. But what is it that has distracted the New Orleans poet while he was perusing this theological classic and that has provoked him to this delightful exercise in trenchant diatribe? Nothing less clamorous than "life and media in the USA, beginning January 6, 2021, the day of the Trump insurrection, ending January 6, 2025, the day of his election certification." Citing instances when Augustine himself turned "wordplay" into "swordplay" by concocting Trump-like fake news, Lavender faces up to the mendacities emanating from our own "city of god, city of / ungod" and draws his own poetic foil time and again. This is serious political poetry, not slogan-ridden protest and not facile denunciation or lamentation, and it wields both scorn and deep insight, thus reviving the spirit of the great verse satirists—Juvenal, Martial & Co.—from the decadent period of the Roman Empire.

—**John Taylor**, author of *What Comes from the Night*

Acknowledgments

Thanks to the editors of these journals and anthologies who published excerpts of this text (in order of appearance):

Jessica Faust at *Southern Review*, 9.16, 9.18, 9.20

Jonathan Penton at *Unlikely Stories*, 16.13 and 16.20

Ralph Adamo at *Xavier Review*, 13.00, 13.03, 13.13, 13.15, 13.17, 13.22

Gina Ferrara for the *Poetry Buffet Anthology*, "museum of capital" (interregnum 1)

Roxi Power et al for *Winter in America (Again* anthology, 22.26

Justin Lacour at *Trampoline*, 20.17, 20.27, 20.28

Peter Thompson at *EZRA*, 6.03, 6.06, 14.26, 15.10

Thanks also to the many poets and friends who read, commented and advised on early versions, especially Peter Thompson, long-time collaborator and friend, whose advice on matters of etymology and translation make me appear much more literate than I am, and Norman Fischer who read the entire monster as it progressed and whose comments and encouragement helped keep it going. And thanks to early readers Cynthia Hogue, Susan Schultz, John Taylor, Rodrigo Toscano, Laura Mullen, Adeena Karasick, Mark Statman, Marc Vincenz, Roxi Power, and Chris Shipman, for blurbs and encouragement.

Thanks to the fam: my grandson Nick for making me feel, again, that maybe being a poet is a worthwhile endeavor, granddaughter Celeste for making me feel the same way about being a punk rocker, and Will and Beth and Ben and Jacqui, who actually make the whole gang a fam, Tycho for his sense of humor, and the triplets—Ada, Freya, and Claude—who were so into this project they elected to be born during it. And, most of all, thanks to Nanc, my partner in crime and my enduring love for thirty years now, just getting started.

Contents

part i (books 1-10)	15
interregnum	138
part II (books 11-22)	145
glossary	338
about the author	352

Foreword

I conceived this project as a spiritual exercise, fitting for a poet of a certain age (by chance, the same age as Augustine when he composed *De civitate Dei contra paganos*), assuming I would find in *City of God* meditations of lyrical beauty and philosophical contemplation similar to those in *The Confessions*. When I actually opened the text, however, I was surprised to encounter a vicious polemic delivered in a tone of cynical derision and condescending parody, reminiscent of the radical right-wing polemics we see in popular media today, like the (ostensibly) new movement of Christian Nationalism.

Coincidentally, I began the reading on election certification day, January 6, 2021, and was almost immediately distracted from Augustine's opening descriptions of rapine in the streets of Rome (during the sacking by Alaric in 410) by images of the insurrection in Washington on TV. The two appalling spectacles of Trump's attempted coup and Augustine's moralistic, hypocritical rant, set the scene for this book, as when I began the writing I realized I was describing both scenes at once.

Augustine's text is purely and directly political, as political as juridical discourse today, for in it he is fighting with all his rhetorical might to bolster the Catholic Church as the ruling entity of the Roman world. His arguments with Cicero and Varro and Plato and Porphyry (among the many others) are carefully and strategically wrought to disprove and dissuade; his concern is neither spiritual awakening nor truth, but simply winning. He is a sort of Newt Gingrich of his time, his theology a playbook for the consolidation of power.

An historical fact that Augustine never mentions directly is likely the most direct progenitor of his text: as he writes the Vandals are building strength in northern Africa, and the possibility of a pagan invasion of Hippo is real and imminent. He is quite literally fighting for his life, as his original title for the book, *De civitate Dei contra paganos (City of God against the pagans)*,[1] makes explicit. Indeed, shortly after completing his magnum opus, Augustine will die in a Vandal siege, and Hippo will fall. Though Rome retook the area (present-day Annaba,

---

[1] The title was shortened to *De civitate Dei* by scholars or scribes after Augustine's death.

Algeria) a few years later, the see was not reestablished. When the Muslims arrived in 698, they razed the city, erasing Augustine's architectural traces, though their catapults and torches were powerless against the textual ones.

My method was simply this: I read a chapter of the Augustine text, then I wrote a poem. Some of the poems focus on the text, paraphrase it, parody it, argue with it, and some ignore it completely. Some are more informed by what was on the news or happening in my life at the time of writing than by the source text, even when I take language from it. Many are drawn from my regular workday in New Orleans.

Conventions: "Double quotes" indicate direct quotations from the Dods translation of *City of God;* 'single quotes' indicate quotation from any other sources, including common parlance, other classical texts, and contemporary media.

A glossary of some of the more esoteric terms and names is included at the end of the book.

city of god

Se pareba boves, alba pratalia araba, albo versorio teneba et negro semen seminaba.

(He pushed the oxen, he plowed white fields, he held a white plow, and he sowed a black seed.)

—"The Veronese Riddle," marginalia from the *Verona Orational*, anonymous scribe, c. 800

part i (books 1-10)

1.01

1/6/21

city of romance
city of law
city of fable

city of souls
ruled solely by
the lust to rule

"earthly dignities...
totter on this shifting scene"
bacchae along the trellis
goths in the garden
"painted barbarians"
bull helmet, fawn skin
boots on marble
hooves on broken glass

we speak of an earthly
and of the other city
and of the enemies
of both

those who flame with hatred
"unable to utter a single
word to its prejudice"

city of granite
city of vapor
walls raised up
in the smoke of war

shrine at the gate

1.02

we persist
in an image
we assemble
as the castaway
lashes debris into a raft
then climbs aboard

how invoke a
god who does not exist?
how invoke
one who does?

1.03

a history of raised banners
pauses for a moment
of rhetorical silence

guardian gods
flicker on the nightstand,
product accumulates

as wet-hoarders
assemble evidence
for the Q conspiracy

1.04

senators huddle
in the stairwells
clutching torn scrolls,
theologians roam the halls

horror film suspense
thumb cocking the pistol

perhaps poets and reporters
transcribe what did not happen?

or "what the truth
extorted from them"?

for what *does* an enemy do
when sacking a city?
(to be sacked is not to fall
alaric recalls)

1.05

virgins and boys were violated
augustine says
temples and great
houses plundered
slaughter and burning
corpses blood and wailing and
not from foreign foes
but from citizens
citizens inside

1.06

the VP *(princeps senatus)*
cut off from above
huddles with his family
beneath a table
lips moving silently
through the litany of jingos
they've been handed
to pray with
while rams batter
the door and voices
shout the most
worldly admonitions
'they're in here'
'bring a hammer'
'give me that crow-bar'

1.07

slaughter plunder
burning and misery
these are the custom,
the novel thing:
that savages show
themselves so fine,
or so says saint
augustine

it was the council
(of rome) set precedent
for the current president
and the ecclesiastical debate
on the ethics and expedience
of torture

1.08

even in this present
laissez faire
distribution of temporal things
a discerning eye
will detect interference
from certain
"third parties"

"stirred with the same movement
mud exhales a horrible stench
and ointment emits a fragrant odour"

1.09

and if punishment falls
to innocent and guilty alike
due to inconsistent
quality control and
poor subcontractor
oversight, remember
our weak citizens

crave wives and husbands
and children and houses and
establishments, for
"the good as well as the wicked...
love this present life
while they ought to hold it cheap"
building the dream
of life eternal

I.II

the beggar at the stoplight
gives a big thumbs up
have a great day he yells
through my sealed window
moves to the next car
donors receive
no special treatment
and they wheel away
swearing off *caritas* yet again
as he mutters
'assholes'
under his breath

I.12

this mortality bus-
iness is ill-omened
at least for those of us
who can't afford
buddhism
but the purple
requiem set assures us
whether laid out
for sky burial or pot luck
on a forgotten battleground
your meat
matters not
for matter complete
with surname and

picture ID
shall be restored
bodies formed anew

1.14

no doubt new recruits
headed for that 'new'
world of democracy
chained in the hold
passing over the highway
of bones
took consolation that the god
of their slavers
stood by jonah
in the belly of the beast
and walked with the trio
in the furnace
without even singeing
his turban and besides
history recounts many who
when washed overboard were
"received on a dolphin's back
and carried to land"
so surely he provides
similar succor for
those thrown over the side
still in their chains

1.16

does the will
remain holy
no matter what
member
intrudes?
so long as
there is no
internal assent
he says

1.17

judas &
all judases
(hardly virgins)
betray themselves
when they rape
the other: a
double penetration

1.18

the sanctity of the body
augustine proposes
does not reside in the integrity
of its components
as there can
of course be
accidents
one might for example destroy
a maiden's virginity while merely
attempting to ascertain it

1.19

for the city is founded
upon a woman's body

flag raised edifice lifted
upon a woman's body

the sacking and the sacrament
upon a woman's body

scaffold rope and pulley
upon a woman's body

lucretia's double homicide
upon a woman's body

I.20

just who or
what may sinlessly
be killed?
irrational animals that fly
and/or creep dissociated from
us
by want of reason by
just appointment by
the creator's decision
to kill or to keep alive

I.21

this innovation of murder
is vexation to the city unless
the current font of *jus imperium*
our DA receive & stand
firm upon his instruction
(whispered from
on high)
just as samson had his
secret alibi, well-
justified in pulling
a few strings
whether by "general law or
special commission"
'our' primary con-
cern needs be to
keep numbers up

I.22

yet again we
entertain the foolish
opinions of the vulgar,
febrile minds
still banging
heads against plato &
the unsinkable republic-

an (quote) majority (end
quote) gerrymandered
around opioid counties
though every vote counts
when the mortgages
on those ever-
lasting mansions finally
do come due

1.23

if envy be
too strong a word
let's just say
he was ashamed

enough being said
about lucretia,
juridical arguments this
way and that
re her suicide
a prudent dissuasion of
cato takes the stage

to forestall
shame with hardship
that the son may
live on like this
"learned and excellent man"

1.24

like job's job, a regular gig
delivers from torment
advances just causes
victories "no citi-
zen could bewail"

but aspirants to heaven-
ly membership forget

they forgot to vote in
the earthly country &
the most high whispers

orders for the secret
mission from the golf course

1.25

"be alert," maiden, for
when the body is
subjected
to the enemy's lust
an "insidious pleasure" might
entice your soul to consent

& even in this
case of a rapist's
fantasy come true
suicide is proscribed
lucretia damned

for lust follows
its own law
and mortal
members
remain as blameless
as the man
who awakens erect

1.26

ah to escape
the ills & enemies
of this life
by taking the plunge
into eternity—
the allure is certainly
understandable
and remember the soldier

is not culpable
for the stupidity of the general
much less the secret
coded whisperings of the
still for a few sweet moments
ostensibly rightful commander
to whom one sort of
swore an oath
back in the day
and as if by coincidence
at this point in the fable
samson again raises
his ugly exemplar

1.27

arguments for
suicide circulate
in the mist
tangled ghosts
camus shakes-
peare the bishop not
to mention antigone
washed in the laver of
time they who
had not the privilege
of their own counsel
deprived of singularity
through iteration now as
dust sweeps across
the page

1.28

following
scribble-track
through the city
in marrakesh lost
in the medina
I showed a street

seller a map
and asked him
to point out
where we were—
he could not

likewise
I can't locate
your *jemaa
el-fna*
on this map
though I could
take you right
to it in the
physical city

I.29

the discipline of
temporal life
these "tottering and falling"
affairs of earth
is school for life eternal
even if one doesn't
live to graduate
even if only
this can be said
with certainty: my god is no
less effective than yours

I.30

why even cybele, mother
of those gods who
do not exist, wannabe
mother of scipio, wags
her finger at your
longing for sensual
pleasures, and remember
the lessons from carthage:

the most glorious victories
turn to shit
for the likes of you

1.31

π eternal ratio
number without number
relation without entity
prior to any thing
invisible yet known to all
governor of gravity
and centripetal forces
and of the human's
relentlessly circular
wanderings

the obverse of π
the prior to nothing
the visible without essence
chaotic energy
of random accumulation
sprawling menage of
materialized ambition
this is
the city

and how could a senator oppose
one he assumes to be god?
not yet knowing how to purify
the heart and seek what is in heaven
or even above
in the city

1.32

drunken celebrations on
gridiron or
battlefield
olympian in scope

prove once and for all
gods are less moral than men
less humane than humans
and if the guns on TV shows are
fake that doesn't mean the bullet-
heads aren't taking actual aim
(says alec baldwin)

1.33

what indeed is this blindness this
hypnosis that plants you behind
a screen as hordes of adderallites
acting on supersecret sub-
liminal clichés stand up
their ladders and drop down in the inner
sanctum? man "even the east" is
laughing its ass off as they trample your
gardens and salt your ground
with microplastics
maybe if you hadn't had it so
easy at the start you'd have been
awake when the first
molotov came through the window

1.35

bless
me father
for I confess
to disappointment
that no
alleviation
of the hobbling
wobbling
dottering &
moldering mental &
physical states
appears to be in the
cards even for

righteous little
me on the way
to the rising
up again
within
my brand new (again)
clothed-in-light
mystical body
but
mortal enemies one day
piles of dust the next
throng the churches
then home to TV
and this is all
ye know in life
here in the earthly
and in that other
city

1.36

and so after shucking
this mortal coil
when the advantages
of this life
that proved so elusive
so strenuous to attain
have fallen just
to those who shucked us
I'll try not to drop
my lyre on your head
like some common
philosopher might
but coil around you
a serpentine logic
the loftiest argument
that ever slithered
out of a tree
and into a city
and so:

2.01

"therefore I do not wish my
writings to be judged
even by you..."
and since you "require
a reply to every exception
which you hear taken..."
well one can't be bothered
in one's inarguably charitable
argument
to attend to every objection
every contestation of fact
one runs into along the way
no time to tarry along
the road to truth

2.02

now let us once more in
mind's eye pat
the hand of the young woman
as she is ravaged ("lawfully"
according to "custom of war")
by the furry visigoth—
for she suffers chastely and
"despite the temptation"
doesn't get into it

2.04

"if this is purification what exactly
would pollution look like?"
the concubine mother of your son
dumped in the gutter so you could
marry a rich tween? how could
any god worthy of the name
let all this happen?
if it were a movie
could you talk about it
in front of your mother?

2.05

now if the goddess-mother were
to know your soul
know what you do
what you think in the wee hours
wouldn't friends and family
blush for you?

unless with the flip
of a switch
she become an adultress
to "entangle you in her deceit"
causing you to lust
for just
what you justly loathe?

try to be temperate
as scipio
so that the senate
lays in your hands
this image of
the double-woman
which you may convey
one day
into the capitol

2.06

the rhetor proves with impeccable
logic that the gods
which do not exist
could give a shit about the city
and let people party at mardi gras
even as the flood water rises

secret messages
whispered in my ear
or is that just
the mushrooms?

but here they come
like every mardi gras
lugging their crosses
by the gay bars
and the boys in chaps
offer up their asses

2.07

it's not the pathos
but the brazen immorality
of the cutter-priests
that plato cannot (theoretically)
abide

but a junkie on a mattress
is the mutilated priest
of our city

basking in god's
"golden shower"

2.08

it is the fiction itself
that poses its fiction i.e.
the god creates
the god
hauls itself
into existence
by guiding
the poet's incantation

"extortion"
augustine calls it—
believe in me
or else

2.09

pardon the "pasquinade" (dods's rendering
of *occentauisset*) but
was ever there such an unblemished
rep more deserving to be taken down?
you praise cicero advocating death
for satirists even as you satirize,
but the longevity of your name will
depend entirely on haloed accounts,
the son you lugged into the garden
who died without mention,
and your concubine, his mother
whose name you will never utter,
sent back to africa vowing chastely
to 'never know another man'
while you lounge in *beata vita*
with the boys in milano

why do I waste my time on you?
your moralism and hypocrisy are
everything I despise, like my
father perhaps, who sent my mother
packing to the dark corners of
her mind while I walked through
the valley of the shadow, and turning
to him received slaps and homilies
(hand-me-downs, all the way from you)

it's a little tough, quite frankly
to pasquinade it away sometimes
but like a banger I
wear your death
sentence with pride

2.10

in the beginning was
the city
and the city

created
morals
rituals of
punishment &
enticement
in a word
god
phallic &
financial
reward
made eternal
no matter
if the god be
or be true
no matter how
entangled the
logic the
logos will net
the citizen
in its mesh
in the maze of
the ancient
medina

2.II

politicians and pornstars
mime the rites as
ithyphallic actors mount
the stage, a phase
that will morph into
church—labeo held
evil gods should be worshiped
evilly, with blood sacrifice
good ones with pot-
luck, milk and cookies
left on the table for
example, so for whom are these
whips and bondage in a cheap motel?

2.13

the syllogism: gods prove
themselves nonexistent
by licentious behavior

ouroboros: the universe
consumes itself
with a pop

2.14

he sits at his table writing
writing all day

when I bring ink or bread and
olives he hands me
a missal and gives the command
without looking up & the
amanuensis keeps scribbling

I see myself
through his eyes
a heap of dirty clothing
something vague inside

from palace to church
to palace I go
from body to soul
and back
carrying the scroll

2.16

so borrowing
gods does have
a history and
didn't begin with pound
or the current craze
for hollywood buddhas
with glamping

retreats and pay-one-
price deals, just like
the monastery at hippo
where all that chaste
spunk spilled onto the
page beside the olive-
oil lamp, quills running
the manichæans through
transfixing the donatists
and lovingly entering the
the hearts of the commoners
well the men at least
necessity of procreation not-
withstanding there were
those who regretted ever
taking breast in mouth

2.16.1

any god worth his salt would
surely have saved us the trouble
of porting over civil law from solon
that trusted sense of fairness and
protection of sacred
wealth magically
writing itself in codex
to save a hypothetical
state from falling into ruin
"while its cities remain uninjured"
roughly what could be said
about louisiana these days
as concealed carry passes and
the saint augustine
marching 100's still
the highlight of the parade

2.17

the city in
its palmiest days

showing
ethics of extremity

it will absorb
a sabine or two
for the city's increase can
come only from others

those who stormed it
those stormed by it
those who hide inside it
those who utilize and use it up
those who do not become it

2.18

sand where carthage once
threatened now a leveled field

tent of the berber
pitched in the cathedral
adjudicating
murder and cornfields
via *jus imperium*

lust for the body of christ be-
comes eternal city
lying in dust

absolved, then
by both nature and law I
pronounce the sentence

2.19

before christ:
the sink of iniquity
after christ:
the sink of iniquity
with the other going down it

not the stammering
of the philosopher
but the thunder of
the oracle
sends down the law
that the quivering pen
translates
into metaphors of the republic

2.20

let city turn against city
let clergy condemn clergy
let laity damn laity, yet
let the law be do what you will

it isn't happiness but
the *kind* of happiness
that distinguishes us
from them (you), beyond
kindness, beyond
any argument, pre-
adjudicated by
lascivious example
delicious horror
the sarcastic wish
becoming the true one

2.22

a cloud of little gods
takes flight from the city
"like so many flies"
from this dead horse

but two millenia later
the selfsame casuistry still
rails at college commencements
and big-box apses everywhere

drone-gods running
cameras and security
while citizens decide
what is most decorous to believe

for despite ancestry
dot com they have
long-since forgotten
the genealogy of their morals

2.23

before the beginning
before word or thing
was the knowledge of
good and evil

knowledge without agent
knowledge without knowing
without voice
without body

next came the
living breathing
manwoman
who conjured the god

manwoman stirring
ashes of what
never was

2.24

like a city
in which the power
has gone out
vague silhouettes
gray on gray
a maneuvering of furniture

shadowy successes
and submissive slaves
deep well from which
the first rumblings of
orgasm come

2.25

from the bone-strewn plain of campania
comes the sound of clashing shields
hooves and hearts pounding
battle cries and death wails
yet not a blade of grass is broken

here the gods set up bleachers
and watch the contest with bob
dylan and special guests until
a whooshing in the air announces
the arrival of khadafy's helicopter

2.26

invitations to profligacy abound in
the cloister, where secrecy makes
the heart grow hard, like
the proverbial blade

here we attend the theater
of the virgin
deity who makes
herself blush
hand under her robe

r-rated matters
explicitly condemned though
too licentious to be mentioned

2.27

the real world augustine
obscures behind his adjectives

we can only imagine
and in this imagining enact
the very lewdness he incants

enchanted thus, drawn to him
for all the "wrong" reasons
we read our history as a priest's
ribald phantasy, last rites marking
the moment of his ecstacy
and our passings as ephemera

2.28

decorative grouper
on the wall of the beach
house in st. augustine, fl.
great red lips
whispering invocations of desire
down past the tan line
and the rich comfort
of cheap wallpaper

a "healthy separation of the sexes"
keeps the neighbors in check
when time to the dawning can be
measured in hours

2.29

TV at 5 AM, insomnia in
one quarter producing
in others absorbing

the theft: stealing coathangers
(one forgets from whom)
the low-hanging pears
to create guilt where
all is permitted

no rousing admonition to
football team, nation, family
god or city can move those whose
temporal advantage has expired

and so "let the current
argument end"

3.01

imagine the dreams
of the berber who spoke
no berber
(for latin was all
the earthly father allowed)

his argument for
the superiority of christ over
the pagan deities he borrows
from cicero's for the superiority
of latin over greek (which in
fact augustine never
troubled to learn
reading his first deity
plato
in translation)

so what might
the slave nanny, her native
language forbidden, have called
the boy-genius's little messes?
urination? defecation?

today's catholicism
might've had
a different catechism
had augustine had
words like pee-pee and
poo-poo and screw

perhaps his penis wouldn't have
been so disgusting if it had been
his winkie, and perhaps if he'd
been able to call the concubine's
vagina kitty he could have also named
the woman herself, and maybe then
he wouldn't have despised himself
for loving her

3.02

like hitler and trump
augustine worries that
his enemies may "corrupt
the people's votes"

3.03

augustine scoffs at
the primitive notions that romulus
was descended from venus
and caesar from mars, though
he does admit the profligacy
of the pantheon could allow for most
anything, including wife-swapping
with terrestrial guys as well as the more
traditional extra-marital & extra-
special inseminations
the simple point being that these
gods are reprobates—they didn't
stand by troy, they fucked
paris over, in-
credible

3.04

but then one *can* make
the argument that
rulers are more intrepid and
attempt more great
things if they believe

themselves descended
from a god, however
false the belief may or
may not be, thus out
of expedience
are the sacred
legends "feigned"

3.05

"the human bed"
tousled, cum-stained
where sylvia got
it on with mars
and founded
rome, unless of
course the sly bitch
made it all up
to save her vestal
ass from being
buried alive, I'm not
coming down one way
or another on the de-
bate just saying it's
a possibility
for as we all know
a god likes to get a little
now and then
happens all the time
about *mare nostrum*

3.06

when manwoman stole
its neighbor's wife
and took what it called
its brother's life

the gods hid
behind a bush

when manwoman cast
the first stone
then cried out
and ran all the way home

the gods hid
behind a bush

when manwoman
was born into the city
and began to discover
sorrow and pity

the gods hid
behind a bush

but when manwoman
left the city behind
and wandered in the desert
out of its mind

the gods came out
laughing and dancing

3.07

now in ilium and rome and
DC we gods deserve
something of a pass
for truly our hands
were tied and not (no matter
what your twisted imagi-
nation might conjure) just
for sex games and not
only by the profligacy
of the populace but
by our own irremediable non-
existence

what effect could our
indignant sermons have
on this physical world
where fimbria and alaric and
trump parade their carnal
triumphs, grasping at pussies and
franchising the piss
out of the porn-flick they
make of the city?

are we to be blamed
for not whispering
loudly enough?

then fuck off
& we'll
be silent

3.08

"at the cackling of the goose"
they came running
cracking the bullet-
proof glass &
mobilizing citywide
capitol police
left standing like minerva
while leftover gods
and leftover senators
swung wide the gates

3.09

if the police are bestowed
like sun and rain and other
taken-for-granted life-
support systems
upon wholesome and sleazy
alike, who can find
argument for the afterlife

in the fairness of their
dispersals? (senators
glide in the halls like
wraiths)

3.10

see here this tooth
the size of my hand
which proves that giants
once walked the land
with crushing electric guitar
and suffering "in proportion
to the size of their members"

while doing archaeology
for me, on the other hand,
it feels most ethical
to ask alexa to select some
easy listening, something
that doesn't distract from the
"furious succession of wars"
that is all we know of history

pitiful gods that
terrify or incite—
enchanted world of
human emotion
the lie of scripture proves

3.11

while
the cuman apollo wept
the human apollo slept
dreaming of sugar and fairies
from his safe house in
the city as
regime changed around him

whether the flag flies
roman or greek
the same old cobblestones
line the streets
and the same bare feet
tread upon them

to stop the
statue from
weeping they
threw it into
the sea

3.12

and so a dense crowd
of gods descended
on the capitol
gods male and female
foreign and local
analog and digital
with briefcases full of cash
and tablets full of laws
and the gods partied down
inviting the senators
to orgies in ex-
pensive hotel rooms
snorting coke
off the bosom
of the goddess
thanks to
a bottomless well
of corporate cash
we were
having a ball
but it was too
good to last
no earthly
heaven lasts

3.14

manwoman goes out
to the harvest
returns with a sheaf
balanced
on its head

stick
figure
wrapped
in a tangle of
thread

hands
like x-rays
of hands

feet
like hooves
broken and
split
by the endless
road

3.15

the flattery of
historians sentences
romulus to be torn
to pieces by his
senators &
the parricide to
accede
the proverbial
throne, but the honesty
of this account
is questionable too
or so says...
sallust, was it?

3.16

for if lightning
doesn't get you
be assured
virgil will

awesome
to behold the
destruction that
rains down
when a
language
is loosed
upon a city

3.18

while the sybelline
books did
hannibal about
as much good
as the bible
did patton
still to the
latter does
the modern city
dweller go
when casting
dice for prophecy
or for profit
for history that
wise old shaman
has learned
to teach most
everyone but
who needs
it most
anything
but what it knows

3.19

as hannibal left behind
a trail of severed digits
to send home those
bushels of rings from
ravaged cannae in the
second punic war so
the french in about the two-
hundredth punic war
left a trail of feet
harvesting anklets
for wives and whores
holding the bishop's words
in mind while swinging:
'love, and do
what you will'

3.20

and the sagantines
bereft and besieged
fell on their knives
threw themselves &
their children into
the fires while gods &
bishops looked on
jerking off, that
is, spewing
sarcasm while
eschewing
irony

3.21

iron bedsteads
oriental rugs
female singers—
these are
the "abominations"
that try the

patience of
our saint
while slavery we
"pass in silence"—
thus the christian
ethic that will be handed
down to lead the expeditions
across the sahara and
across the atlantic
and across the wastelands
of eminent domain
to the capitol

3.23

dogs leave their masters
and roam the streets
horses, mules and bovines
forsake domesticity
latins, too, turn cities
into battlegrounds
urban warfare
strife unto itself, but
also as augur
for the age of qanon

3.24

a ploughman
following a mule
framed by laurels
is the logo of
handy kennedy

gracchi's efforts
continued

3.25

for the work of discord
built the temple of concord

in massachusets as well as
agricento, and probably
in arkansas as well
where the little town
(pop. 244)
has a killer
football team (the
pirates) and the grownups
worship john deere
except sometimes
when the mortgage is due
a mother wakes up yelling
that she took off her
boy's cleats and found
a pair of hooves

3.26

civil wars
and servile
enacted
in the city
code & archived
in the child's
kleptomania

pithy
sayings and epic
narratives join
the liar's pact
to create consciousness
as advertised

life modern &
otherwise
bitter
for this
toothless hag

3.27

do bloody
wars prove the
gods inept
or just thirsty?
marius & sylla
filled the city
with corpses avenging
this or that out-
rageous slaughter,
libation for
the battlefield dogs,
gods & senators
licking up the
millennial mess

3.28

cities on
the auction block
like farms

marius marries us
to the cycle
of revenge
and the vestal
fire flickers out

3.30

when oxen spoke
when fetuses
whispered from the womb
came christ to the city

when serpents flew
when livestock &
women changed sex
came christ to the city

when earth actual earth
fell from the sky
when it rained fire and stone
came christ to the city

when the sea boiled over
when the capitol was buried
in cinders
came christ to the city

when locusts fell
into the sea
when the bishop returned to africa
came christ to the city

3.31

manwoman walking
across a desert
sees a dot
on the horizon

an oasis
it thinks
a garden
a gift
of some god

salvation
succor
sustenance it
salivates

but it is only
a city the
city of
no-god

no
salvation no

succor no
sustenance no-
thing

manwoman stands
before the gate

4.01

I have spoken
of a city of
god but I have come
to the city
of no-god to
retell a story
misapprehended
these two
thousand years—
and to the god
whose existence this
work disproves:
vigilate maneat vivit
your time may come
after all

4.02

I don't remember
leaving you
wounded
by the roadside
where you
would never
be found

today a city
stands where you
breathed your last
the earth
you tasted

has been paved over
and traversed
by a million souls

here in the wet
cement of a new
walkway
I place
a star*

4.03

to be good
to be wise
to be happy while
rolling in blood &
slaughter or
(same thing)
perishing the
thought, turning
away in horror...
for the rich
lie awake "anxious
with fears, pining
with discontent"
while the poor slob
happy with his "modest
estate" pats his
belly and the wife &
kids look on roundly
no need to
mention the slave
whose rolling is
literal in this conceit
of which the principles
are of
course nations

4.04

if an empire
is a robber gang
with the "addition
of impunity"
what is the
church
what is
the city?

4.05

a "long succession
of dying men"
held these offices
until the offices themselves
died
and emperor
bishop
gladiator
concubine
catamite
all statue-
sque concepts
eventually
evaporate
like the flesh
of their bearers
and do not
rise again

4.06

stunningly brazen
these robber
princes like the as-
syrians pick the god
to trust in who cedes
the most land, every-
thing from

here to libya
turned into moneybags
and the slaves
to carry them—
it will be a few
centuries before
crosses appear
on the banners
and the crusades
really get rolling

4.07

look in this mirror
and if there's an ounce
of shame left
in you blush
for the heroic
deeds of your
bloodthirsty past
and these pitiful
gods you spent
your chintzy
offerings on

4.08

so the porter
that "everyone"
sets before their door
takes the place of
three gods
but cloaca, goddess
of outhouse
trysts, can't stand in
for three guys
no matter how
deft her fingers

4.09

jove himself
shows his
vanity by sitting
for the sculptor—
better gods we worship
without image

4.10

thank god the real
virgin birth can put to rest
the vexing venery of
venus versus vesta
no matter how good
a movie it might make, that
long chain of begats
funneling back to
the belly-button-less
fall, divine seed
that sprouted sex and
language

4.12

it doesn't take a rocket
scientist to figure out
that smushing a beetle
isn't stepping on god's toe
for the world is not god's
body but someone else's
someone base, fallen and
broken in the falling:
manwoman

4.13

for how if
I am to keep my
sanity can I

imagine that this
slave I am whipping
(while whimpering)
is part of a god?
& what god
could possibly be
profligate and
licentious as the
concubine who lies
(and writhes)
under me?
and so god is
almost certainly
not human

4.15

happy nations
coexisting like
the houses
of a city or
else waging war
like gods might

4.16

for a thunder-quoting
orator the objects of your
ridicule appear to be
simpering plebes and their
equally simpering (bumbling
slapstick) deities, imaginary
enemies upon whom you
rain imaginary fire
and ash, just as I
you, our defensive
sarcasms
righting the great
wrong in writing
(or vice versa)

4.17

such faith in language
to counter every argument
to stop every hole the effort
endless as killing
flies or feeding nations
thus the length of the volume
for while you borrow your
stodginess from plato
you lack his concision
and must drone on
and on for centuries
ridiculing your own dreams

I dream tonight of a pestilence
a gross expression
from a wound on my neck
I am embarrassed and try to hide it
wiping the pus on my pants

you were 70 when you finished
as I am now, only beginning
how do we die then?
will it be together
or apart?

4.18

felicity street in new orleans from
s. claiborne to magazine is
a river that runs through many
nations carrying the smelt and
ore of fortunes up and down

junkies and bankers wave
to the passing floats
impassive gods
on the prows

ships not of state but
of the continuous flow

manwoman in all
its variety
indistinguishable in
identical costumes

4.19

was it the "feminine loquacity"
of the goddess that made the
statue speak, or was there a
guy in drag inside holding back
his giggles? it takes extensive
knowledge of history and religion
to deride gods and men properly
as the rich son derides
the father, source of his wealth
reminder of his own inability

4.21

one ought to
be content
to throw all those
gods and goddesses
that both verity
and vanity disprove
into the vortex with
virtue and vulcan
and the whole crowd
of etymological
puns and just
go ahead and
get down with varro
whoop it up in
the language
a bit

4.23

beating the dead
horse of felicity?
the barrage of rhet-
orical questions, the ironic
why-not's finally dragging her
into the capitol where we can
once again phantasize she
might be getting it on
with earthlings? did her
name sound like fellacity
to you, hilarious
sex in the city? the air
full of demons that brush
against your skin in
metaphorical massage? but
god still gives the best
felicity, not at all like
"licking a painted loaf"

4.24

can we blame this æther-
full of false gods simply on
the drunkenness of our fore-
bears or is there a logic(os)
even here? do the rhetorical
flourishes that push the
winged shadows into
the language suffice to
describe the difference
between gods and concepts?
or are we hanging
plato out to dry
on this one?

4.25

we take for granted that jupiter
gave lousy felicity, too busy

sneaking into the boudoirs of
human wives and of course
there was that "beautiful boy"
attested by more than one
(lucky) eye-witness account
god porn calling up imagery all
the more concupiscent for being
vague, an art film of sultry
bourgeois women bored and
hungry for a little god-play,
the boy grecian with
laurels and grapes,
ah who can turn away and not
look back at the flickering
projector light of manwoman's
imagining

4.26

vacationing through these
last few days as a living
being I visit the *museo de
arte de querétaro* and stumble
on you again, not on the walls
but carved into the very
structure, your cast of motley
pagans capstoning the arches
of the former *claustro de
san agustín,* founded in 1728
to stage the salvation of
the *indios* of the high plains
and the silver
under them—
on the upper level a troop
of angels holds up the cornice
drain pipes extending from
their mouths like great probisci
for sucking the blood
of men and women
and phantastic animals

4.27

god of the poet
god of the philosopher
god of the politician

rule of the first
is profligacy
of the second phantasy
of the third totality

here the west is reborn
psychic pantheon
stood down by casuistry
and the 'right' of *jus imperium*

bare desert imagining
itself garden
out of which, delirious,
trump wandered

4.28

it is "irksome" but apparently
necessary to relate
the childish failings of one's
opponents, no matter how
like wisps of smoke they be

just think how things
might have been
had christ been atop
the transom when alaric
came knocking—
even if failing to quell
the rape and plunder
this perfect pol-
itician's god provides
eternal escape from
the smell of rotting corpses

4.30

gods of the nations
that balbus babbles
about, christ sent
packing with wit
and whip
taking no
pleasure of course
with either
for it is wrong to
desire, to desire is
to be wrong

4.31

if we could just get
god's surname right
we'd have a nation
which could lay waste
its neighbors, a patri-
otic undertaking
"even the rabble"
should get into
while demons yee-
haw in the æther
which indisputably proves
the mutability of the soul
and the eternal reign
of the imageless
sword

4.32

telling lies about gods would be
of course a very efficient way
to seed a city with market units
for dates mangoes and finely
woven wool—augustine here
foreshadowing both marx
and the opioid epidemic

in clear-eyed self-critique and
(fleeting) textual
pleasure, should anyone
doubt the prescience
of his word

4.33

ergo the ego:
soldiers of fortune
become soldiers of god
contradictions and puns
chalked up to the laughable
ignorance of the enemy
while the vagaries of fortune
are tallied as mystery
and the crusaders' banner
(southern cross or
stars and stripes, pick
your favorite movie) still
stands above the smoke

4.34

am I jack nicholson in *the shining* typing
inanities over and over while going mad
and freaking the daylights
out of the *femme fatale* and
possessed child? well one can find truth
albeit accidental in such pagan texts
as may fall out the detritus of memory
and anyway it never hurts to insert a footnote*
(*for augustine's innovation is not only
casuistry but academic scholarship)

now at the end of the fourth book the berber
takes up the jews, who worshiped the image-
less god and did okay (parting waters,
great sex) till they decided
to kill its carnal visage (i.e. 'son')

thereby launching that cruciform shadow
that will hang over the west, symbol of
faith hope charity torture and
dominion until I (at the very least)
lie down finally among the mothers &
the fathers

5.01

of twins

one twin may turn east
the other west

one twin may be good
the other evil

one twin might be temperate
the other drunken

one chaste
the other tumescent

one discerning
the other blind

one joyful
one morose

one bathed in eternal light
one shrouded in darkness

one conquering, triumphant
the other broken and enslaved

one male
one female

one by the thread of what it can
never be: the same

5.02

"a single act of copulation"
under the stars
yields different horoscopes
thus twins prove
christ eternal by
coming untwinned
leaving it to god
to lug the logos
into the capitol
in 2021

now at the gates of the city
manwoman presents itself
straightening cuffs
in a mirror
taking the hand
of its image
skeletons in formal wear
holding out their card

5.03

the potter was broken
on the wheel of her metaphor
an ego (i.e. faith) more fragile
than the pots that are thrown there
(and tabled at the craft fair)
but twenty centuries and countless
rotations of the celestial spheres
later, horoscopes still make
the paper and geminis
and libras alike take notes
(for propensities of course
not precision, shapeless lump
from which the well-rounded
identity will be spun)

5.05

mathematics, a "vain science"
especially for those concerned
with equations of fate, i.e.
my twin is not my multiple
but the primal absence
of me, proof positive that
the prick that rises on
this fantasy of doubles
is anyone's but mine

5.06

21/8/16: taliban casts out aryans

we are never within
but like priests
always outside
the struggle, dis-
interested observers
of twins in conflict:
left vs right
male vs female
laic vs secular
spy vs spy
city vs city
augustine vs lavender

5.07

"oh, singular stupidity"
to choose a wedding day
under these auspices
letting the evil twin follow
the good one out
hanging onto its heel
releasing into the æther
yet another
demon shade

5.08

you may have thought I was
fond of cicero but in case any-
one get the wrong idea this
morning I'm ripping him a new one
we can't have my own
metonymies turned against me
what I call father you calling fate
causes fatal embarrassment
and when I blush
my arguments bloom

5.09

who speaks
when fate speaks?
will of the true god or
spirits of one
kind or another
for the wind is called spirit
but since it has a body
it is not the spirit of life

spirit of foreknowledge
spirit of contrition
spirit of speech

5.10

the fact that god foreknew
what you would put in your will
doesn't mean you didn't write
it of your own free one (&
in sound mind of course), for
who exactly would have
dragged you to the table
put pen in unwilling hand
and ouija-scripted every
curve of every letter?

5.11

it might be vanity to stop
the argument at this point and raise
voice in simple hymn of praise, cata-
loguing nouns by the dozen, each
a metonym for a dozen more, from
stones to veggies, brutes to angels,
seeds and forms, beauty, health,
fertility, heaven, earth, even the capillaries
of the "smallest, most contemptible
animal" mapping harmony and peace
like the veining of a leaf

5.13

is it in the court of public opinion
or before god that biden pleads
the ethics of giving these poor
afghans back over to sharia
enforced with AK's?
when tossing the baby over the barbed
wire is the best hope for its future
a moral argument to boost morale
of the voters is a difficult catch, even
for such an exceptional american

5.14

or perhaps devout catholic
biden knows from augustine not
to court fleeting human praise
seeking the afterlife "in the mouths
of admirers" in this earthly city of
kabul, where "the dead are succeeded
by the dying" and the taliban
keep racking up points in heaven—
keep your eye on eternity, joe

5.15

nobody's perfect, of course, so
it must be the most virtuous of
the nation, those who resisted
avarice for the sake of the commonwealth,
who "despised private affairs
for the sake of the republic," who consulted
in the spirit of freedom, addicted
to neither crime nor lust—
it must be for these earthly
virtues that we are rewarded with
earthly success, honor among nations,
great literature and the right to brand
our law and our language on
most everyone else

5.16

except of course the city in the sky
which has no room for terrestrial
do-gooders, only for those
who do nothing but gaze nobly
upward and light a little incense
when the bodies under
their feet start to stink
for the upturned nose points
to heaven and to life
eternal, where no one dies
and no one cries, and
muhammad even installed
houris

5.17

augustine would have frowned
on his godchild muhammad's
insertion, for the pleasure
of the principles, of the female

in the city of god,
though the sharia he could
have penned himself

5.18

a bit of a trick
to puzzle out
the ethics of god
handing the jews
over to rome
(as we hand these
women
over to
the taliban)—
perhaps pro-
leptic punishment
for the famous
lynching?
though *we*
don't have
like god &
brutus to kill
our own sons
in homage
to an earth-
ly city
(way easier
to get into
heaven
than to fuck
with local politics)

5.21

the god-terminus
yielding to necessity
just as
the god predicted

they have closed
the curtain poorly
and through the crack we see

choir boys
helping the priest dress

5.22

america's longest war didn't
quite match the first punic
which drug on 23 years
and doesn't even approach the
samnite which had a golden
anniversary before they took a
breath to count corpses
so all things pass,
and fast,
in the twinkling of a sentence
one war's over
and another begins

5.23

god made short work of radagaisus
a hundred thousand goth bodies
left bleeding in the field or carried
to the auction block (slaves going
for a penny or less in those days) while the
romans went home picking their teeth
bragging of zero casualties and even
fewer casual graces (the essence
of nobility) thus were the worshippers
of demons subjected to the "true
religion"

5.24

it might be tough
to distinguish
in the dense underbrush

of this prose
much earthly difference
between the christian
emperors and the other kind
but rest assured they rested
in felicity and had warm
feelings for justice even if
implementation was human
(all too) and they left
about the same number of bodies
strewn on the plain as did
their faithless predecessors

but when the shadow
docket instates the texas sharia
their pictures will be on the walls and
ours won't

5.25

constantine & gratian grace a
paragraph like a sumptuous table
set with empty chairs, far
from the slums of the city
of humans they ruled, why they
even named a city after c.
(constantinople), leaving gratian
to fend off eternity
for himself

5.26

"more by prayer than by sword"
was eugenius beheaded (figuratively
speaking) and a christian eugenics (quite
literally) sown upon the world
and the prophet in the desert
jovially handed over
jove's golden thunderbolts
to the taliban while god himself

huffed and puffed and turned
their own missiles back at them,
and in a lesson for
the millennium theodosius for-
got he had promised mercy to
the thessalonians and chopped
them up anyway but did his penance
so piously the ladies of
the court wept to see it
so all was forgiven

augustine here cautions anyone
who might wish to argue with him
not to, lest "garrulity and vanity"
spin down to satire and levity

6.01

indeed it does stand to reason that
any god who can't (for example) plug
that leak gushing crude into the gulf right now
is probably going to be ineffective
at patching up this aging body and/or
soul for eternal life as well, unless the plan
has always been to let the species, like
the dinosaurs, fizzle into an oil slick
saving for eternity
only me

6.02

"wandering our own city
like strangers," says tully
but never mind rick
steves will get us around
cicero having forgotten
in his discussion of the academics
that he was in fact academic
at least in the great
academy of the city

knowing every god bridge and tower
and feats attributed to each
by such as varro

manwoman strolling the ruins
book in hand

6.03

the white quill
dips into the well
returns to the parchment
imitating with minute pre-
cision or exaggerated parody
markings on another page
that being varro
and cicero beside that

augustine's version
posted to the scriptorium
biblioteca capitolare
in verona a century
later to be copied
and a translation of a
copy of that copy
I now translate and
copy out

this the provenance
the look backward

to gaze at eternity is always
to look backward

6.06

so excited is the translator by the notion
that eternal life will never be granted via
a netflix series that he switches to thee
and thou and -est, at least

at the beginning of the chapter (even as
augustine spends a paragraph on the subtle
differences between the fabular and
the fabulous) though he forgets himself
and goes back to talking like me and you do
in the second half, not that
I can really talk about inconsistent registers
(as thou, dear reader, knowest well)
but a. also spends a minute talking about
proper translation of μῦθος as *fabula* &
not *mythicon*, arguing with etymological
fervor (as only someone who does not
speak the language can) for slight advantage
on the current enemy (still varro) before
the death blow in the final sentence

6.07

poets write and
people perform
what gods desire them to
and what more condemnation
do we need of these lowlife gods
except to say they admit into
their orders "mutilated and
effeminate men" which not even
harlot choirs will sink to, augustine
being well-informed on admission
requirements into either, makes
theater of their theology

6.08

even depraved men, under torture (as
depraved men often find themselves) refuse
to admit they aren't macho, which proves
there is no lower form of sinner than
a sissy, and no less credible form of god
than a goddess, the ultimate test of rigorous
theology being a vigorous phallus, or at least

the pretense of one, despite and disregarding
last night's gambols in the cloister and
what remainder might be found
in the beards of the prophets

6.09

the city is a mirror in which
the mime rehearses and the new
husband spies on his maiden
wife atop the giant dong
of priapus, a theater with scenery
as dense as demons in the air
manichæan *raiders of the lost ark*
bathhouse graffitti come alive

6.10

the dome of the capitol
is mosque to the god capital
where senators like seneca enact
civic theater & cynical theology
i.e. we who worship
what we censure, do
what we condemn, adore
what we reproach
make a forum of fakery...
who else
could be our god?

6.11

for thaddeus conti

"the conquered have given
law to the conquerors" said
seneca of the jews, likewise
you brought order
to the squalor of the city
even as it shoved you

handcuffed, into the back of
the big white van

the rule was that you
gobbled up every
drug in the house and then
sang out the bakkheia

this is the law, priest
this is the law, police
this is the law, poet:
do what you wanna

I have faith, t.c., that you'll rise
from your ashes at the cheapest
crematorium in town
and be crowned
with laurels, soccer-mom
houris pissing on your chest,
lawmakers, senators
fanned out below
waving like sea grass
to & fro

6.12

& what is felicity but power
dominion over one's minions
(slaves of course don't count)
the arrogance of immortality

manwoman playing
toy soldiers in the sandbox
makes the doppler sound
of an incoming missile
purses lips for the explosion
sending sand and soldiers
flying with screams of agony

"there is no greater death
than when death never dies"

a pause for meditation

& it resets the tableau

7.00

in which we continue to ridicule
"depraved and ancient opinions"
that to this day influence the un-
enlightened, whom I am called
to save from their error and put
on their knees, however revolting
their presence may be

for "unclean spirits" course
through the writing, serpentine
genetics older than adam
visible (inescapable) in both
motive and accident
slip and intent

7.01

augustine accidentally
(with the best of intentions)
deadnamed the imageless god
θεότης and manwoman thought
he was talking about
someone else which
caused some awkward moments
like the septuagint scandal
the treaty of tordesillas
and january 6 2021
but time heals all
and after a brief bit
of it the faux pas
was quite forgotten

7.03

today's modern
manwoman is unimpressed
by your catalog of things
gods can't do, but
it will take the forms of
your jokes and turn them
into hilarious sendups of
blacks jews and
italians

what changes
over time:
not the believing
but the meaning of belief

7.04

manwoman taking in
the roman
sites feels a little
shiver down its spine at
the ancient grandeur
and then from all
the way across
mare nostrum
searing wind
of the scirocco
you can actually taste
the saharan dust

7.05

"that which is contained being
signified by that which contains it"

as wine takes the shape
of the krater

master of signifiers

scribbling day
in day out
in its office
in the episcopal cloister
in hippo regius
(today annaba) in numidia
(today algeria) in the maghreb
(today lots of things) in the
sahara in north africa in
the western roman
empire—

thus is the signifier
contained

7.06

with the help of god
I'll design a god
to designify god

correct an error
with another error

split an arrow
with another arrow

with the help of god
I'll leave my husk
clinging to the tree
and emerge with wings

7.08

I wake this morning
thinking of my father
sitting at the kitchen
table writing his memoir
on a yellow legal pad
with a yellow wooden pencil

left hand curled around the work
so I can't see

then I remember:
the dead
however they be clothed
can't write
what they don't recall

7.09

it is almost as impious
to believe that jupiter
impregnates itself
as to believe it doesn't
though janus appears
capable
of both at once

7.10

thus janus and jupiter
make four
gods suspending (for the sake
of argument) disbelief in
each other to illustrate the logical im-
probability of the anti-
quated theses under-
pinning recent
personal injury case law (*jus
imperium* again) cited by trump's
attorneys to keep him from having
to speak: the
ex post facto ex-
executive ex-privilege

7.12

calling jove pecunia? ridiculous,
what use would this om-
nipotent motherfucker have for cattle, no

matter how rich the cut? or the meto-
nymic cash (with which he would
buy exactly what?) it's not like he has
an episcopal manse to pay
insurance and utilities (no taxes
of course) on or anything
the point being I'm saving you from
yourself when I shove the image-
less god down your throat, passing
the plate with the other hand
so that you'll be as rich
in virtue as you be spent
of silver

7.13

if the forgoing has not convinced you
of the "absurdity" of primitive notions and
self-evident genius of genesis and
amos then I don't know
what will

manwoman certainly
bought in, held st. george's
shield for two millennia (so far) even when
einstein showed it a magic sword that made
banners and shields evaporate

7.14

of mercury and mars
this is what we know:

mercury is speech because
speech is the messenger
that which
goes across

mars is the cold air
that enters the house

when the father comes
home smelling of
sweat and cordite

these are their
stars

7.15

"but why has janus
received no star?"
and venus such a bright one?
while jupiter's but a
pin-prick? they've made
metonymies of our metaphors
says the sceptre
just ask hollywood about
reusing lapel patches
from auschwitz
ask them why
it's still venus who
shines the brightest

7.16

diana moved to indiana
in the form of kat von d
forsaking city
for a manse in the woods

once the remodeling is complete
she plans to again pick up the
quiver and continue the work
her goal: a single sentence laying
down the law for everyone, a rebus
inscribed across ten thousand bodies

"they will have her be a virgin
because a road brings forth nothing"
adds augustine, and two millennia

of catholics have a laugh at "them,"
though they of all the mohammedans
must admit, virgin birth *does* happen
now and then

7.17

varro himself didn't believe
what he was writing
augustine contends
some god was holding
a gun to his head
for as any platonist knows
there is a subtle difference
between belief and believing
for example varro might
believe that saturn
was jupiter's parent but not with
the absolute certainty we have that the
"universal mass of nature is governed and
administered by a certain invisible and
mighty force" and that luke skywalker
is indeed darth vader's son

7.18

"even the acutest men are so perplexed"
at the obviously anthropomorphic origins
of the other side's platform with its glaring
omission of what we're going to use
to bridge the gap that abolition opened up
especially now that demokracy itself
sits about three tiers below the google-
zuckerberg terrace in the trickle-down
economy and begging for a little
highway money seems blasé to these
who helicopter to the office anyway
but there'll be time to lament the state

of the roman road tomorrow
today I'm doubling down on bitcoin
tip from my contact on the inside

7.19

after a time, so it is
said, manwoman got tired
of eating its own seed
spilled on the ground
and started rolling in the dirt
with saturn, from whom it
learned to appreciate jupiter both
orally, palpably, and linguistically
and in that cloud of saharan dust
they kicked up it was tough to tell
the human from its gods, a
confusion which still reigns today
in certain primitive cultures

7.20

exactly what should be damned
concerning the mysteries at eleusis
remains elusive, even mysterious
as varro chalks it up to fruit harvest
and a. merely transcribes, adding
a bit of etymology but lacking the usual
punchline of condescending sarcasm
which makes me wonder if this one
didn't cause a wee bit of tribulation—
did the fingers tremble around the
quill at the thought of dissing this
particular rite, which even plato was
taken with?

7.21

down at the crossroads
"rites of liber were celebrated with such
unrestrained turpitude that the private parts

of a man were worshiped in his honor"
the giant member loaded on a car
and wheeled through town to its place
on the dais where a local matron crowned
it with a wreath, an event so salacious
augustine must use aporia to pretend
not to describe it, likewise I
will never tell how much fun it was to read

7.22

it's funny how the closer
we approach to death the
less worrisome it is—existential
promontories are a young man's
game, old farts like me and
the bishop more concerned with
pissing themselves than with eternal
life, houris or none, indeed
the prospect of world without end
seems like unending tedium
as tithonus found out
to live forever might actually
be what they call hell

7.23

I almost feel sorry for poor
varro, having to endure from his
crypt chapter after chapter of aug-
ustine's cryptic bile, I mean the
bishop will work a conceit for
half a page just to poke fun
at one of v.'s slips of the tongue
none of which matters one whit
these days, both hands retired to dust
augustine with his
name on a few towns and orders
wins, and varro, first one
dead, must take it lying down

7.24

last night, walking through the
broken streets
of this broken city
I grew inexplicably anxious
and began to run

it's been a while since I ran but
it came back to me even
easier than I remember
I'm not even winded

glad to have on
my good boots, to
dodge the cracks and
jump the potholes

I was in new orleans of
course but the city
felt old as annaba

when I wake I lie still
and work to remember

7.25

augustine praises varro not
for his writing but what he leaves out
in this case the story of atys's
castration: "our varro has very properly...
been unwilling to state it"

a., on the other hand, is not so shy
and must attach the parable to
the one he is currently mutilating,
association by language if not by
fact, tried and true
republican strategy

7.26

"these effeminates, no later than yesterday,
were going through the streets and places of carthage
with anointed hair, whitened faces,
relaxed bodies, and feminine gait"
like bourbon street, no later than
last night (it's sunday), where a good
sampling of roamin' man and
roman (trans) woman normally debark
upon the perilous shores of romance
too drunk to think quickly, deadnaming
themselves in a stammering
search for anonymity straight
through to confession
this morning

7.27

"...he who worships with such things... twice
sins against god, because he both worships
for god what is not god and also worships
with such things as neither god nor what is not
god ought to be worshiped with..."

logical fallacies to make
a phallus droop

does the not-god
have no-phallus?
and how ought
a no-phallus
to be worshiped?

as aught?
as naught?

even a good god ought
to be naughty
now & then

7.28

lying with my woman
doing puzzles on the bed

I slip into a dream and
it is as if I become
the city around us

I take its shape
its iron structure

my map reflected
in the torchlit sky

my limit
and the desert beyond

I kiss her
on the belly

7.30

there is no proving
creature from creator
but in sorites, the heap

as plato zeno &
quintillian understood
a single grain of sand
will never make a pile

but drop the sahara
on their heads &
they will notice

7.31

beyond the ability to catch the occasional
gorgeous sunset or tranquil mountain vista
"what benefits god gives to the followers"

beneath the specified income bracket
up to and until date of death
shall not include health care or pre-k
nor a whole lot else beyond this
tent under the bridge and paper
plates of cold stuffing from the center
on thanksgiving, though rest assured
that after death the cornucopia
will be spilled upon you

7.32

"...men who understood what they spake
and... men who understood not"

it is the translator who genders
this line, for augustine it
goes without saying:
quosdam scientes, quosdam nescientes
some knowing, some not
what comes out of
their mouths and pens

all words
are the other's words

all flesh
the other's flesh

quosdam scientes
quosdam nescientes

7.33

"malign spirits"
glide in the æther

in the curve and
curl of the letters

word made flesh &
flesh made text

7.34

numa had himself buried
with his books in his arms
but when the ploughman
dug them up twenty
centuries later the senate
found the tomes "...unworthy
not only to become known...
by being read, but even to lie
written in the darkness..."
and ordered them burned
(except secret copies
saved for the elect)
the word
twice born:
once in exhumation
once in guile

7.35

the hardwoods have already
been logged from this
hillside, the second
or third planting of paper
pines have covered it again
and the little pond
is black from the
needles

I stare into it
my childhood
nekyia
and a wavering god
looks back

romantic nek-

romanteion
of a white boy's arkansas
I wave
good-bye to

8.00

thaddeus, again

you kept the membership
at st. francis xavier catholic church
a secret from your shamanic side

I imagine cab rides home
still tripping, straight
to the pew beside your mother

you once owed me twenty bucks
and brought an entire gram
the debt must never be

canceled you said
something must always be owing
one way or the other

8.01

for debt is fundament
of desire, the lie
of desire, desire
große lüge
that which is
wanting and yet wants
not, wanting naught
but to be wanting

knot
of desire
I shall not
return to

8.02

manwoman as particle
of the not-god

not the hive mind
manwoman as

one who did not
walk the grecian earth

but turned a page
upon the grecian dust

8.03

"indeed, it were tedious to recount
the various opinions of the various disciples"

to put it in writing—
what isn't said
what is denied
just that

8.04

what I say
augustine says
plato says
socrates says
is that the city
imprisons those
it desires
to hold close
and after the lynching
puts up a statue
names a street
after them
norman francis
christ gandhi
or laâbi

liberty & equality
motto of the fraternity
of slave traders

8.05

trump beside the plane tree
at mar-a-lago
discourses during covid
on the pharmakon
splitting up the world via
a new treaty of
tordesillas while melania
dabbles
in NFTs
(which he confesses
he hates, pre-
ferring the sub-
limity of the dollar)
but advising the republic on
democracy, conjugal ethics &
probate law is only
half the job, there
remains the yin-yang a.i.-
compiled fractal gerrymander
to keep the heavenly
manchins sound

("...and those also who have been
ashamed to say that god is a body...")

8.06

insomnia at 3 a.m.
far from imageless
devils and pinwheels
course in the darkness
& my lips form
the famous
three words

memories of
my father raging
in dementia
my mother alone
in her last days
lifelong friends
gone or going
what emptiness, what
suffering awaits me?
vanity of endeavors
no human thought
can succor
as I lie in state
looking up

god help me

8.07

"...by what eyes of the flesh have they
seen wisdom's comeliness of form?"

what image might be borne
of the imageless in mind's eye

seamless blue sky
of logos or

wet-draped form
of athena
through the wikipedia
keyhole

shadow on the cave wall

8.08

drugged on the pharmakon
blessed by the absence

of ethical misgivings (slaves
and women manning
the fans) lobes focused
on the "greater
good," plato may be pagan
but he's our first
love, our reference we've
never read, our reverence
for reverence sake

8.09

a coalition of greeks
and just a couple of
berbers will save
the philosophical filibuster
and protect the nobility
from that rabble
of punic voters
as war approaches from the east
yet again

8.10

the poem
that never
got written—
forgotten
as soon as it
was thought like
a tuft of marsh
grass up-
rooted in a storm—
now floats
freely on the waves

8.11

"I am who am"
plato the sailor
off to egypt

to read some glyphs
and make some more
just might have
encountered genesis
along the way

8.12

platonic plato
plato that never was
wash your hands
of this business
these christians with eyes
on the horizon,
peripatetic academics
walking on
mare nostrum
towing back
on a tiny golden
thread (a miracle!)
boatloads of slaves,
their work ethic
will serve them well
for what unfathomable effort
what storm-tossed seas
must be crossed
to set up those new
markets in the west

8.13

plato precurses christ
along with augustine and my
old man when he bars
poets from the republic-
an party (though he does
leave the door open to reconsider
if one would ever come out
for voting restrictions)
for the silent majority that

will never drag a finger across
a page of unwrapped text—
on the way to church one
sunday poppa warned me
'there's no money in it,'
I countered with
spiritual quest, purifying
the language of the tribe, feeling
things more deeply, etc., stuff I'd
read in honors english (the only
honor I would finally find) &
felt I'd won the fight (& we loved
to fight) though went on
to fail even at the quest
for failure, my mini-
scule vote that even then
wasn't counted

8.14

I wonder if augustine
when referring to those
"obscenities of the theater"
foresaw netflix or if he
was thinking more like
judge judy, with whom,
come to think of it,
he has a lot in common...
if only those forever
rules of time and the cœnobium
had not prevented a
hookup, we can just imagine
the power-couple they
might have made in
modern media, love
and do what you
will, says he to his dom-
inatrix, and those little
devils in front of their TVs
fidget in their seats

8.15

but don't make the mistake
of assuming, as so
many do, that these
demons on the air
are as elevated morally
as they are in the
ratings, for even that is
theater, a "fiction of
the poets" and it isn't just
climate change that's putting
those malibu beach houses
under water

8.16

it's easy enough for
a professional orator to dis-
prove the subliminal logic
of an apuleius or a roger
ebert as they rank their
shades of the æther
but manwoman still
walks on terra firma &
still buries its dead there

8.17

manwoman felt (more
than) slightly embarrassed (πάθος)
that after worshiping all
its gods and after casting
out all its demons,
after all its platos and
christs, all its
buddhas and muhammeds,
it kept on
dying like the low-
est most contemptible
insect, like the most de-

crepit dog on the road
and in its impotent intellectual
struggle got so mad (πάθος) at
itself it went around slashing &
hacking everyone it ran into
until at last it lay down
exhausted
in the carport of its enemy

8.18

2/5/22

pathetic
apuleius thought since
no god has dealings head-
on with manwoman
he could use his magic
touch and bribe a rep-
ublican to take his petition
straight to mar-a-lago
where the "god of socrates"
literally sits
but someone (anyone)
distracted the messenger with
an unchaste woman just as
putin and xi jinping were
shaking hands in brasilia

8.19

it is a "pestiferous and
accursed doctrine" that teleports
crops from one field
to another, something not even
apuleius would brag about,
but piously silent monsanto
christians needn't send demons
to keep a finger in
every furrow, since the mystic-

al omnipresence of the one
true god keeps
the royalties rolling in

8.20

2/6/22

"no god has intercourse with man"
leda and semele might vote
for a gender-specific reading of this
theology, but who in their right
mind would want to go hopping
from supplication to supplication
sneaking around and playing
both ends against the middle like
these conniving little devils,
hired lobbyists of the æther
skimming the 'legitimate political
discourse' off the top
of each transaction

8.21

the big question being
do the poets pick up those
"corporeal indices of mind"
well enough to read god's
silence? or shall we take plato's
word, from the
podcast, that
it's just more static
in the æther?

8.22

so every syllogism and every
metaphor point
to the fact that gods
which don't exist
can't be trusted to protect us

from the lies they don't tell
about either putin or global
warming (if this winter's storms
don't prove once and for all that
climate change no more exists than
the demons who cause it)

8.23

oh to return
to those golden days
when we were clue-
less enough to take
this bullshit seriously &
imagine in our nar-
ratives a golden age
that might have been
nostalgic to fall from

augustine remembers fondly
hermes trismegistus's
remark that manwoman
shaped out of clay the gods
that created it, predicting
the rise of
augustine and his christ
in "mournful prophecy"
of the eighteenth century
slave trade

8.24

sadly though
manwoman lacked
the leisure to grow
expert at "this
art of making gods"
and had to count on
mystical transformation
to make its lumps of clay

remind the supplicant of
circe's hair
though a few
millennia of practice did yield
a pretty convincing
some said transformative
trump troll doll

8.25

2/19/22

putin fires a couple of cruise
missiles across the ukrainian bow
causing that mother
ducking with her christ child
a mere artillery shell
to wonder if she should dodge
east or west

biden exposing
the *großen lügen*
from the east
floods the airwaves
with his own

cyber-sabers rattle
from who-knows-where
(invisible threat like
demons in the air)

meanwhile
in kyiv it's ice-
skating and cafés
as usual while pundits
ponder yet again
on their podcasts
war's curious provenance

8.26

"but it was the grief of the
demons which was expressing
itself through his mouth..." for
the exponential explosion of sepulchres
would have foreshadowed a dire
shortage of rituals had not god
created a class that couldn't
afford them and further
relieved the pressure with
sky burials and those
bulldozer graves
that pretty much pave
eastern europe

hermes the foreteller
said it all years ago
but then we have to wonder
with augustine
if it was really that great a leap

8.27

but let us as
new conflict (the last?)
approaches
in eschatological sanctity not
confuse the "*ornamenta
memoriarum*" we hang for our
warriors with those our enemies
drape over theirs, for god
sees neither
race nor politics
excepting ours,
and in its plans
for the end of history forgot
to include itself
just like
the rest of us

9.00

2/23/22

beside the other's
fire another dances

shadows, rhetorical
mise en scène

dollar signs flicker
by crypto candelabra as

now at the border of east & west
language is turned back

and they've shut off the gas
in case anyone gets ideas

9.01

"included under the name 'gods'" these days:
1) the lover's gaze (distracted
just now by a [figurative?]
mushroom cloud on the horizon)
2) language
(suddenly entranced
with itself in the mirror)
3) Q, anon he (am I
making a leap here?) slips
below the intelligence
quotient of even his faithful
fans (not necessarily a bad
stratum to aim your gerrymander at,
here in the interregnum)
which leaves us to wonder
with augustine's ideal reader
"whether the worship of a number of gods
is of any service towards obtaining blessedness
in the future life" i.e. if playing

the numbers game pays
in the end, which might seem
to the uninitiated to be just what
plato is saying, though putin threatens
anyone who might have another god
before him with olympian
fire, so expedience may be
the better part of logic here

9.02

as the tanks roll in, israel hedges
its bet and declines to call
the kettle black

europe cancels (well,
cuts by 10%) the re-
curring oil buy

pulling SWIFT codes causes real pain
in the porn sector: xi jinping to the rescue
with a wholesale wheat buy

here's hoping the good
demons get the goods
on the bad ones

9.03

"their mind, as apuleius says,
is a sea tossed with tempest,
having no rallying point of truth or virtue
from which they can resist
their turbulent and depraved emotions"
much less combined ground and air
attacks from three sides at once
and street fighting in kyiv

with the west to his
west and the east to his

east, zelenskyy
gives men (only; there's a limit
to equal consideration) between 18
& 60 tokens for a free AK and revokes
their passports, sends women and
kids underground and notes
that his collaborators in democratic
theater have left him rather
on a rock in a firestorm,
prompting biden to jump in with his absolute
sternest demeanor and cut
putin's allowance in half
never veering from
"the path of wisdom and
law of rectitude"

9.04

even a stoic
three or four
levels down this
tale within a tale
will turn pale
and pukey
and wax
peripatetic
when ship of
state begins to feel
the sea under it, &
where is the shame
in that?

9.05

augustine notes it
isn't the passion (πάθη, he says,
though he speaks no more
greek than I do) to
slaughter one's neighbor one
ought to be ashamed of, but

the inability to keep that passion
restrained, chained in the dungeon
so to speak, deep in the bowels
of the capitol where senators
need never tread, even if the
occasional ghostly howl
makes its way to the chamber

9.06

"the mind of the demons, therefore
is subject to... a hurricane of passions"
& these many heads of single mind
are ill-equipped to intercede
between us and our maker
when the air-raid sirens distract
and the subways are so
crowded it's hard to think

9.07

it is, once again, to the poets we owe our
confusion of these low level func-
tionaries and the real string-
pullers above them—

beyond the lares and larvae the
real god

beyond putin another putin
dangling a marionette,
beyond biden another biden
with an r.c. remote—

which explains why
they feel not
the arrows of our insults &
they don't die when you blast them
but resurrect (there's a box-
full in the back room) and

like the green knight await
patiently next year's
appointment

9.08

I was trying to decide if that image of
you falling off the roof was memory or
movie or dream
or perturbation of demons
flaunting longevity to us
mortals, or indeed if it makes a dime's
worth of difference which sort of
phantasy it is if you're not here
to share it

9.09

monday, 2/28/22

today we are prepping
carnitas for fat
tuesday—anyone
who wants to
please stop by

then on ash
wednesday we
always go vegetarian
(maybe a little fish)
it feels
healthy, this leftover
ritual

next week it's
back to work
installing solar panels
though some cust-
omers have elected
to postpone installation

given current price
volatility and
supply chain interruptions

9.10

plotinus comments rather
wryly that man-
woman got lucky
when god made it mortal
unlike the demons
who remain saddled
with bodies,
however transparent, e-
ternally

9.11

apuleius on the
other hand contends
we turn into demons
ourselves when that im-
mortal part of us
lifts into
the æther—
"lares if they are good
lemures or larvæ if
they are bad, and mānes
if it is uncertain"
rise from the cool-
ing corpse
to become next-
gen intercessors

9.12

but perhaps the most
convincing arguments for the
immortality of the soul
are put forth by my
friends annie

and danny as
well as my brother jerry &
my sister fay all
of whom
passed from this
mortal coil
some time ago
yet continue to post
status on facebook

9.13

likewise @augustine
updates its opinion
with each new translator
the social media
of early-modern digitization, i.e. the
army of scribes scribbling their
fingers numb playing eudemons™
online hoping it will one day go
viral even as @a
points out certain glaring in-
consistencies, holes in the logic
board

9.14

"it is a great question among men
whether man can be mortal and
blessed" (*beatus*) and perhaps the ladies
too ask this question as they board the
last trains out of kyiv leaving their
men behind to intercede with
putin's tanks, for zaporizhzhya has
fallen and while the endgame hackers
have darkened a few screens
the queue of souls up-
bound from the fields is
approaching the interminable

9.15

3/6/22

the city of god
is to
the city of man—
augustine, master
of analogy, points out—
as the kharkiv of a week ago
is to kharkiv this morning,
perfect apartments and avenues
vs. piles of smoking rubble,
commuters who rode the subways
vs. living there

& since neither biden nor macron
proved up to the task of mediation
it falls to christ
to intercede &
welcome the flood of
refugees across
the border to their
new life of
eternal bliss

9.16

"the gods, if so minded, might mingle
with men, so as to see and be seen,
hear and be heard"—is that what
all the clamor's about? egos
like college professors demanding laurels
consummate with their rank?
or do they come like whitman's
jesus and walk, pallid, with the
wounded to the border?

like theodosius (see 5.26 above) putin
has no recollection of promising

anyone anything and shells
the 'humanitarian corridor'

tit for tat, mcdonalds and
starbucks shut down
moscow operations (the ruble's
taking a nose-dive anyway)—
fingers crossed the resulting hard-
ship causes the
tyrant to think twice

9.17

city of god
is to
city of man
as logos
to alogos
as the aetherial
branches of the tree
to its chthonic root
as the clear light of the dream
to the drear shadows of the real

9.18

oh "aerial demons set between
the ethereal gods
and earthy men," strafing
apartment blocks and reactors, bombing
this morning in mariupol
a maternity hospital, as we
lift off from this earthy plane
please intercede for us with
whoever's on duty
from here
in humanity's
gutter hear
our plea

9.19

manwoman running
across a heath
mad with grief
tearing at its rags
leaving this trail
of its divestiture:
golden miters
broken vases
brass buddhas
and multi-
armed shivas
snake gods
minotaurs
apollo and kali
loa and christ
imaged gods and
imageless
gods with names &
gods whom never a pair of
lips shall utter—
ivory trinkets
decorated with glyphs
fall around its feet as it
empties its pockets
sobbing in self-pity
crushing every
insect in its path

9.20

"...resembling the demons in pride
but not in knowledge"? or have we
entered a new phase?
δαήμων, *daímōn*:
power-knowledge, heat-
guided like the missile...

gas prices soaring in california
prompt an outpouring of
caritas for kindergarteners
positioned under the bombs,
the saint javelin emoji
goes viral raising a million
plus, zelenskyy('sexiest
man alive')'s tik-tok feed
is off the charts with
swooning women,

& at the polish border
mother courage still
searches for
her children

9.23

3/13/22

"I will not spend strength
in fighting about words" even
if putin *is* giving fifteen years
for refusal to tweet fake news
(can't wait to see what he &
trump cook up for the species in
'24) and you can see this morning
from poland the red sky over
yavoriv and hear rifles cocking
all over europe: natural signs,
not language

10.01

"philosophers have wasted their strength
and expended their leisure" pursuing
"happiness" in whatever language, but
the cult of the colony will super-
cede agriculture and cross an
unfathomable sea, from manes to Q,

latreia to latrine, your worship
on shipboard piously praying each
matins for safe passage of cargo
& crew (indistinguishable but for skin-
tone) through a sly slip of the tongue
(your becoming my) starts the slaves
worshiping the god that enslaved
them, & a new world awaits strikingly
similar to the old one

10.02

4/3/22

gods, daemons, angels and humans
all seek "that certain intelligible light…"
all seek "to receive illumination from
another" and let that other speak
through them, through quill or macbook
or tongue or tongues, that blesséd
feeling of possession, nine points
of the law that tickle men and
women and assist all of us to
get our nut, though outside
kyiv this morning russia in
retreat proves all possessions are not
created equal, that men possessed
by conscription notices grow tired
of seeing their friends and feet
blown up quicker than those
possessed by that devil-may-care
attitude that comes from seeing
your children slaughtered &
possessions burned, and putin staring
down the barrel of his personal
firearm in the glow of a phosphorous
bomb outside the window starts
to babble in a language no one
else can understand

10.03

I walk down the porch steps in the
pre-dawn, past the azalea bush,
chard and tomatoes in the raised bed,
and, distracted by a lizard scooting along
the rail, press a little button in my pocket
and hear my truck chirp once,
twice

the beggar from 1.11 still limps
by the curb at norman francis &
tulane, & all along my foggy
way to the job, over a wanly
ironic neo-classical theme that
seems to imply the human com-
edy for all its blather is
still worth a chuckle or two, npr
hosts a discourse on
the city of god vs. the city of
reality, and I take dictation
in mental shorthand

I stop at a pj's to grab a latte
and earn a star (ten stars means
a free coffee, extra large excluded)
and meditate in the line on how
the video game of the world economy
is as bloodless and savory as
mortal kombat, & then
gods and warriors and scenic
serenades lift with the fog
upon the workday

10.05

"thus, that sacrifice which he says
god does not wish, is the symbol
of the sacrifice which god does wish"
i.e. the bloody animal

on the altar signifies
the "contrite heart"
in contrived submission

and the butcher of
aleppo steps forward for
our next lesson
in semiotics

10.06

one can under-
stand for a moment
but then you name
it and it is lost,
says manwoman of its
enigmatic pastime

10.07

"glorious things are spoken" of
new orleans &
lots of other cities
aspiring to be god's
with well-dressed people posing
in front of churches
for the tourist brochures
but
in case you haven't noticed
truth and happiness don't really
mix, if you want to be
happy trust in god
or lithium but leave truth
to the pros, those who take
pride in knowing
all hope has been extinguished…
that's a new orleans tradition too

10.08

seed the barren wife gave birth to,
son not even a prolific woman
could bear, or a flame that ran
between the divided parts, when
angels predicted sodom with its fire
and salt, when moses from the yoke
in egypt struck, when the magi suffered
wonderful things that they might be
vanquished all the more signally,
magic arts, incantations
demons are addicted to
whereas moses, dealing out
miracles, delegated upon pharaohs
plagues, waters which could not
be drunk, manna descended,
worms and putrefied flesh,
birds filled the camp, turning
appetite to satiety, enemies
to god's people, swallowed up
alive by the earth, serpent sent
in punishment, symbol of death
set against death
by this serpent
preserved in memory
afterwards worshiped:
"tedious to recount
the ancient miracles"

10.09

"he [porphyry] complains of this through the mouth
of some chaldæan or other"

I have seen her, now, several
times, working the narrow
median at city park and canal,
not old but sun-weathered in her
weathered sun dress, left arm lopped

off above the elbow, the brown
stump clutching a brown bag
to her side, right (only) hand lighting
a cigarette, or trying to, unable
to protect the bic
from the wind, and
out the window this
time I hand
her a five, which she wads
into her palm behind the frus-
trated lighter, and she says 'jesus
loves you you know' and walks off
between the cars, still
snapping the bic, showing her
rotten teeth at every
window, saying 'you know
jesus loves you, right?'

10.10

now just as those little
demons who in bygone days haunted
the airwaves put on angel
wings to fool poor porphyry
and his "well-disposed chaldæan,"
so the tucker carlsons of
this world stir up band-
width calling devils angels and
angels devils, fooling the most
of our noble but gullible cit-
izenry who then consider themselves
the wiser for filtering out
'fake news'— well, jumping on your high
horse calling kettles black
has long been the preferred tactic
of preachers and cheating
husbands, and will continue to be so
long after the donbas and russia and
usa all the way
of chaldæa go

10.11

new orleans jazz and heritage festival 2022

do the "fumes of sacrifice" rise
over those distant fields so tourists in
sunglasses and hawaiian shirts can
fire up a doobie and dance in this one
to the hot 8 brass band, big freedia
& the fabulous cimafunk? it is the same after
all dirt under foot and when pete townsend
helicopters an e-minor the volume likely
matches a shell hitting close by or a
javelin taking out a tank down front,
all in all to a bored god looking down
from on high the microscopic writhing
cultures must appear pretty similar
and the difference between the
odours of cordite and cannabis or
bar-b-que and cremation might
seem negligible to that deity not part-
icularly invested in the sensory
universe dancers and
soldiers cling to so dearly

and what does it say of a god
who views such struggles
with equivalence? (we ask,
with augustine,
with porphyry,
rhetorically)

god, held
to an older standard,
to a judgment of
the judgeship
hears hymns of praise
from the gospel tent

10.13

"the sound which communicates the thought conceived
in the silence of the mind is not the thought itself"
for the physical is the fallen
presence denotes lack

that which walks walks hobbled
that which speaks remains unspoken
that which falls falls with language

10.14

I'm off to pick up some
"earthly necessaries"
checking my phone for the list

when I dream about chard
chard ads appear on my phone

when I think about augustine
hooded figures

the death that never dies

devils running
back & forth
between
phone and
phantasy

10.15

"and so it has pleased divine providence…
that the law enjoining the worship of one god
should be given by the disposition of angels
but among them the person of god himself
visibly appeared, not, indeed, in his proper
substance, which ever remains invisible
to mortal eyes, but by the infallible signs
furnished by creation in obedience to its creator

he made use, too, of the words of human speech
uttering them syllable by syllable successively
though in his own nature he speaks not in a
bodily but in a spiritual way, not to sense
but to the mind, not in words that occupy time,
but eternally, neither beginning to speak nor
coming to an end, and what he says is acc-
urately heard, not by the bodily but by the
mental ear of his ministers and messengers
who are immortally blessed in the enjoyment
of his unchangeable truth, and the directions
which they in some ineffable way receive
they execute without delay or difficulty
in the sensible and visible world
and this law was given in conformity
with the age of the world and contained at
the first earthly promises which symbolized
eternal ones, and these eternal blessings
few understood, though many took a part
in the celebration of their visible signs,
nevertheless, with one consent both the
words and the visible rites of that law enjoin
the worship of one god,—not one of a crowd of gods
but him who made heaven and earth, and every
soul and every spirit which is other than himself
he created
all else was created
and, both for being and well-being
all things need him who created them"

10.17

manwoman sits
in its desert, eyes
on the sky

eyes that number
as the stars

god made man-
woman to have
these eyes so someone
could peek at him
behind the curtain; 'to be
is to be
seen,' he says,
'I need these
eyes to exist'

but manwoman was
confused:
for eyes it heard I's
and turned its gaze
inward...

I's that number
as the stars

10.18

I came to new orleans
from the gray-green hills
of arkansas
to make my testimony
which I have called
the city of (no) god

my research took me
to a cemetery
where people of all
religions, my an-
cestors among them,
lay together, in the
same crypt even, & in
perfect harmony

long hours
days & weeks
in my cell

and here, finally,
you have it!

undying gratitude
to my brothers &
sisters who read
the numerous
early drafts and to
my wife who looked
after my failing health and
to my children who sup-
ported me even as I neg-
lected them and to my
colleagues in capital
who lent me the leisure to
devote myself entirely
to this work while others
worked streetcorners
begging alms from
passing cars

I apologize
for its length—
I know your
time is valuable too

may you
have the strength
to see it through

10.19

5/9/22

putin celebrates the
end of one war with
beginning of another, "for
that which they take pleasure in is not
as porphyry says... the smell of victims

but divine honors"
all those burning bodies
just to light the runway for
an aging punk-rocker
to hock grandiose *lügen*
at the ec-
static crowd

10.20

"thus he is both the priest who offers
and the sacrifice offered"
lying down on this table in
sadean glee, here I am,
eat me, eat this mad
christ that parties down
the centuries, I am the way,
the am that I am, the shot
of vodka with breakfast,
morphine on the battlefield, I'm
the rule and the forgiveness,
I'm the invisible worm, the
greener grass, the good
thing the neighbor always has,
the quiet confidence, the lack
of fear and trembling, ab-
solute aplomb in front of
the camera, I never stammer, I
speak impromptu and it
sounds well written, the
way the truth the light, all
that, that's me, that's the
me, the me that I see,
the eye that I don't see,
I of the storm and I
of the norm, smell of green
pastures, mirage
in the desert, dis-
turbance in the air

10.21

"the power delegated to the demons...
this power is found to be not merely harmless
but even useful to the church, completing as it does
the number of martyrs,"
so putin is finding out, as the norse gods go
flocking to nato just when he thought he was
getting tough on opinions, losing
votes even as he gains ground

porphyry, however, adds that "a good god or genius
cannot come to a man unless the evil genius
has been first of all propitiated"
i.e. christ follows dionysus, his bride-
nuns were maenads last night,
chastity makes them cum, for how
does one repent who's never tasted
blood?

10.22

"it is by true piety that men of god cast out
the hostile power of the air,"
hard to say if this is referring to russian
air strikes or circulation of the corona virus
either of which seems to demand
a procession of saints to the front
praying with laser-guided precision
an air once empty imagined full
now filled and imagined empty but
for inert machines & engineered
viruses, which helps us imagine
imagined demons might have
physical claws, might strafe a
village or shut down a school system,
hands without bodies, managers of
the imaginary:
"we who are polluted by sinful flesh
should be cleansed by the likeness of sinful flesh"

10.23

porphyry, no doubt, "spoke according
to his light," while *we* "are bound
to speak according to a certain rule"
that certainty of rules being why we
can speak at all, and also why god
happens to exist, that is, the rules god sent
down are the rules that created it, a
feat of proleptic engineering
perfected by an unknown scholar/
scribe, long before copyrights &
patent law

10.25

numbers thrive,
come alive, is this
the quickening,
is it the end?
a shadow like
a storm
on the horizon,
petrichor,
a different charge:
we will change!
we'll be wiped out!
at last!

10.27

these days they
are filling
in the potholes
with broken up bits
of the city
robbing peter
to pay paul
as they
say, but gravel
under one's

bootheels in
this part-
icular moment this
is god this
is logos

10.28

your apostrophe to porphyry
is ample demonstration of your knuckle-
rapping ability, rhetorically
speaking, and could such casuistry
be the genesis
of the genitive?
if not the genital?
is to name you you
to possess you or
be possessed by?
does language owe its own-
ership to a patriarch traceable
back in the abstract to
a primal semantic land grant,
the big bang of meaning,
when bits of world
and us were first bitten
off and salvaged
from savages? well, we'll
say what I want & you
won't be talking back
save through the mouth
of some future (br)other who'll
own the both of us &
the land we lie in

10.29

the same way my mother
embarrassed walking
in on me in the bathroom
christ makes the platonists blush

with his carnality and his
specificity, there being for jesus
no ideal unnameable, only the one
bodily instance and the swear word,
and this despite the fact he taught the
hebrews in greek, romans as well,
thus forcing augustine to learn an
etymology or two even if he left
the language itself to actual apostles
and the punic rabble running
round and round the tower while
manwoman, in this instance a
simple laborer, carried on
carrying bricks

10.30

"...that souls should desire... to come back into this life, and to the pollution of corruptible bodies, as if the result of perfect purification were only to make defilement desirable"

for the purest desire is desire
to upend purity, all desire's
desire to defile, and no
incredulity can mask the slaver

10.31

5/24/22, uvalde

"If, then, the soul has always existed, are we
to say that its wretchedness has always existed?"

wherever foot has trod in dust
a print remains, describing the weight,
direction, and ancient wounds
of the soul who left it,
illegible signature,
illegible yet memorable

2nd amendment rites:
male maenad's
ar-15 portending
the city will be sacked

'why her? why my beautiful daughter?
she always brushed her teeth,
she made us things, she made us
pictures and little arrangements...?'

final responder
st. ted de la cruz
gives the eulogy at
the nra convention
but cherubim in louisiana
may now carry pistols under
their robes... pray for them
that their thoughts
remained chaste
without lust for revenge
or desire for personal pleasure
that eternal bliss be theirs

10.32

chained to our post in this earthly city
(city of romance, of law, of fable, etc.)
shadows of the logos
(exxon, disney, amazon, etc.)
play upon the walls

"...a kingdom
which does not totter like
all temporal dignities"

porphyry's fatal
error laid bare,
vain argument

made venal
by vain faith

city of lust
city of larvae
city of domes

my graffiti wall
my stone tablet
my white plume

by the lares shrine
hands reach out
for alms

wind of the sahara
wiping away footprints
of the caravan and
the tribe it carried

interregnum

I

museum of capital - for norman fischer

the city of god is a painting in the
museum of capital, which lines the walls of the capitol—
you can tell the difference because the o looks
like a dome, my 4th grade teacher told me, a few
years back, though the capital with an a attempts
to swallow the conceptual field by encircling
the building with its city meaning, as opposed
to its rural ($) meaning, where you might say
monsanto takes the place of town, having found
a way to charge interest on capital it never had, never
even had to borrow, seed money, so to speak,
growing from nothing to feed the world, somewhat
less bucolic than *agnus dei* days, at least
here, in america, and it wasn't that long
ago I was in the italian tyrol up the hill
from ezra pound's castle, we were taking
the funicular to the restaurant at the top
and just as we were pulling into the station saw
in the almost vertical pen beside us a little lamb
who looked up & baa'd as we passed and we said
how quaintly european without it occurring to our
quaint american consciousness till we got inside
and looked at the menu that she was it, reified, fet-
ishized object of market forces, listed at 'market price,'
fluctuations being too volatile, apparently, to allow
the number to be committed to print, a ghostly thing
like the ownership of the grain that fed her
and her mom, for ownership grows increasingly
abstract as the capitol dome gets more and more
often misspelled, and we paid for her abstractly, with a card,
never noting the actual price, just up the hill from where
the author of 'with usura' came to lay his head, still
hard in those days, on the cold castle stone, after

his daughter mary bailed him out of st. elizabeth's,
before the author of 'kaddish' made his pilgrimage
and the hard head softened, pulled down its vanity a
bit before sighing its last, now as certain as he had
been of his place among european capitols that it
had all been a botch, which of course it was...
and I keep looking for similar conversion in my current
fascist object of inquiry, i.e. augustine, who likewise
had a pretty line or two but was way more comfortable
spitting *simultas* than *caritas*, or indeed the current benito
wannabe getting botoxed in mar-a-lago, de facto capitol
of capitalism, lavish museum to its schmaltz, but see no
signs of conversion (unless in the language of capital we
mean by 'conversion' 'theft') in either, in which clever
referential fashion augustine proves himself correct
that the city of capital will always surround the capitol &
though the city of god may hang on its wall there will
be a price tag on it

2

from: C___ K___ <————-@gmail.com>
to: B____ L___ <————-@gmail.com>
date: Jun 3, 2022, 7:01 AM
subject: Update (at long last)
Dear Mr. Lavender,
Here is my update re: City of God (thank you for your patience):
First of all, thank you for trusting me with this assignment [to annotate the poem]. Respectfully, my conscience won't allow me to undertake it, because within your very interesting writing style you seem to be reflecting that 1/6 was an Insurrection, and also that Pres. Trump instigated it.
I strongly disagree with this idea. I try to get as close as possible to truths and facts by not simply accepting the current government's pronouncements, and instead by researching those and other sides to the story through the best well-sourced and responsible writings I can find.

I feel like I am then protecting the freedom of my own
mind as well as defending America's hard-won freedoms,
in a way that brings some real clarity to a lot of fog.
If you are interested in pursuing that kind of fog-
clearing, here are some suggestions (there are others).
Review Articles in Archives (starting 1 yr. back or so), @:
Revolver.news
https://thenationalpulse.com/topics/news/
TheGatewayPundit.com
AmericanMind.org
HumanEvents.com
Again, thank you for the opportunities you have given
me, and very best wishes to you.
Sincerely,
C____ K____

3

marrakesh, 2008

marrakesh, *amur (n) akush*
ancient berber name
slurred through centuries

some say it means
blood-red earth,
some say city of god

a cobra rises from a basket
in *jemaa el-fnaa*
filigreed fingers reach out
for tips

stench of burning hair
from the tanneries

side of beef
draped on a moped

imams sing to each other
tower to tower
like cicadas
here in the spring
but the old ogress of the folktales
still whispers charms in the alleys

outside the medina
half a dozen soldiers in pressed
khakis examine a blueprint
spread on the hood of a jeep

and across a hundred meters of
barren red desert
the new city sparkles
like a mirage, disco balls
and sequined gowns, piña coladas and
bikinis pool-side, cold beer and
hashish, air conditioning, camel rides
for the kids,
easy airport access,
granada, for example, which
was once ruled from here,
only a 2 hour flight

4

dear st. augustine—
last night
I dreamed my dick
was huge like liber's,
hard as rock,
standing above me
like a totem...

I am fascinated with
its touch and cannot
leave it alone but
just as I am about to come
someone walks in the room

and I try to cover it up...
I can't, of course, all
I can do is hug it to
my breast and she
pretends not to notice
as I furiously blush

5

in 1970 on campus at u of a I ran into
a high school buddy I hadn't seen for
a while and we sat down to coffee
in the commons—had I accepted jesus
christ as my lord and savior? I had to
shake my head, and so with
sad expression he pulled a napkin
from the chrome dispenser and drew on it
with his bic pen, two cliffs with a gulf between them,
such as wile e. coyote and roadrunner
might jump in the course of their famous
perambulations, a span the roadrunner
could easily clear but which would send
the coyote, after a dramatic moment
of suspension, to the distant floor below,
and these two cliffs my old pal labeled
'god' and 'man'
and to complete the rebus
he drew a sideways
cross spanning between them
and the cross he labeled 'jesus'
explaining that christ is
the mediator, the bridge from man to god because
of the cross, and I said well the cross
really isn't that good a bridge is it
because of that cross-member sticking
up, do we have to jump over that?, and
it's a good thing they didn't hang
him or we'd have to walk a tightrope,
and he said I shouldn't take the
symbols so literally (had he

read augustine on
the literal and figurative?),
likewise
augustine names the bridge, the godman:
"for it is as man that he is the mediator
and the way... the only way that is infallibly secured..."
christ's victory over sin and death
as certain as the roadrunner to make the leap

6

vacay, july 2022

at liberty university, lynchburg, virginia
the mission is to 'train champions
for christ' with courses in "the scripture
which is called canonical," as well as aug-
ustine himself, & certainly not in the rites
of liber, though the jerrys falwell did
exorcize some rights for example
jr. in the front pew cheering
becki getting her nut atop
the hired libertarian dong,
taking liberties with ladies
and the language too
until the breaching
exceeded the preaching
and the heir
fluffed up his hair
and retired
to focus on the trump campaign

7

7/12/22

the webb space telescope
sees back to a time before
christ, before trump even, before
giants walked the land, peeking

over the cosmic cliff,
while we vacation
at chilhowee campground—
20 years ago we hiked one day
20 miles in the pyrenees
but today I'm wheezing and
sweating in my hiking
boots while youth pass
us in shower shoes, and back
at the camp sucking down
beer and aspirin under the
trees under the marvelous
blue sky, and a deer, a doe,
comes to stand in the bath-
house door, chewing its
cud

part II (books 11-22)

11.01

psittacine citizens
practice city zen
trafficking language
under the i-10

sojourner, nomad,
washing in a plastic bin
outside the tent
as day begins

11.02

scripture that predates writing—
authority that predates authors—
rapine that predates predation—

the city is neither
future nor past—
ever and
never present

11.03

august 2022

rites of late summer
enacted by the select committee
raving "in the incurable madness
of impiety," qanon sha-men
turning coat on the stand, better
part of valor after a taste of
actual jail, high tea mid-afternoon
while the populace heads to
mcdonald's, tucker
carlson in the earbuds

11.04

what we see
of the city is
the gulf between
the we
and the see,
the braille
in the sidewalk

11.05

"eternal knowledge of
eternal time"—
for language
sets its own clock,
as easily
eternal as
anything else

11.06

there can be no time
without a creature to per-
ceive it, and no creation
without a time
of creating,
but who created
that first alarm?

11.07

"for the knowledge of the creature
is, in comparison of the knowledge
of the creator, but a twilight," he
notes, foreshadowing darrow's
argument in the scopes
trial, where creatures
argued creators upon
"infallible scripture" in dayton,
tennessee, july, 1925, an

eternity ago, yet a time
brought crisply into focus
by even our crude optics,
twilight of the idols,
someone said, and yet...

11.08

in theaters we applaud
that lazy seventh
day, when "god's rest
signifies the rest
of those who rest
in god," i.e. those who
can rest period,
& the rest of us rest
with the oxen

11.09

angels, "having
never been expatriated"
need neither
creation nor cremation, but
every other creature
must have its day, its
history, its
provenance &
its ending

11.10

the trinity

a cup may lose its liquor,
a body may lose its color,
he says, but
the trinity has
nothing to lose

an air may lose
its light or heat,
a mind may lose its
wisdom, but the
trinity cannot be divided
into what it is and
what it has

three points &
three segments make
this simplest
stable structure,
which braces the roof
over the ass & the
walls around the child,
it keeps the hay dry &
the child king

those whose aches and
infirmities cause them to grow
impatient for
"the incorruptible body
promised to the saints
in the resurrection"
may take comfort
in the trinity

and augustine adds this eleatic
caveat to former friends,
the manichæans:
"this world could not be known
to us unless it existed"

II.II

a conundrum:
why did some angels,
suffused as they were with
perfect blessedness and
eternal life,

choose instead
to follow the path
of darkness and death
that is
the city?

because by then,
despite what
everyone says,
they had already
fallen into language

II.12

I wonder if
"those first men in paradise"
felt as beat-up after that
first day as I do after day
one digging in the garden,
or if, like movie stars or
super heroes they could
till forever and never
get tired and never
glance over their shoulder
at the crows on the fence
waiting for the next
seed to fall

II.13

to be
"delivered from all dubiety"
to "eternally abide
in the same enjoyment,"
the proud jouissance of
immortality, eternal
return be-
coming eternal
coming...

private pleasure
too intense
for certain angels
who fall
into the crowd,
into the conflagration that is
the city

11.14

the devil's guttural tongue
resists rhetorical analysis—
his glosso-
lalic under-
standing under-
cuts the human—
gasping for gods
in the gutter

11.15

the exorbitance—
elliptical orbit represented,
for simplicity's sake, as
a circle, augustine's shak-
ily-drawn aureola
in the blur of the lacri-
mose beholder's eye
while the camera obscura re-
cords a crooked finger
wiggling an ominous c'mere
to those first investors
in the colonial slave-trade

11.16

"more is often given
for a horse than for a slave,
for a jewel than for a maid"—
a brief lesson in economics,
inflation in the natural

order, forces of supply and
desire,
for don't men
cattle and swine
put themselves
on the auction block
all the time?

11.17

neither nature nor nurture
foretells this future
in which
the orchestra
plays mozart as
its audience sinks

11.18

god with its
excellent eye
setting world in aesthetic balance:
for every dishonor
honor, for
every evil report
rosy readings, for every
rich a thousand
poor, for every unknown
a hundred un-
questioned certainties,
for every deception
a guiding light,
for every peter
a paul,
"as it were
an exquisite poem
set off with antitheses"

II.19

"obscurity is beneficial"
especially with the
große lüge
on the line

II.20

light is good
darkness bad
unless you're nursing
a hangover, and
who isn't?

II.21

"...what else is to be understood by that
invariable refrain, 'and god saw that
it was good?...'" but the architect signing
off, *disinterested* analysis of
structure and finish,
rigidity of beams,
trueness of corners,
triangulation,
impermeability of roof,
resistance to wind

II.22

architect, builder, ruler
dreamer and visionary,
you who lay the bricks
and you who formed them,
when you are gone
the city will not notice,
of what you thought
you created you
were no more than
an eye among others,
sensory node

at the end of a tentacle
swaying in the current
flowing over a reef

II.23

the body is
an address, a
cell in the "house
of correction,"
fleshy prison
where essential
being is detained

II.24

city rising out
of protoplasmic swamp

tracks of commerce like
the trails of amphibians
through water hyacinth,
tails dragging
in the mud on the shore

what visions I have
in the rising vapor

II.25

how naturally
the rational
evolves into the moral,
the natural
eye atop the
tetrahedron,
rotating above
the fog

II.26

"for how can he be happy
if he is nothing?" asks
the original scholar &
master rhetor, leaving that
third term of the en-
thymeme unspoken,
to be happy, then,
be something

II.27

augustine further affirms:
"the very fact of existing is by some natural
spell so pleasant, that even the wretched are,
for no other reason, unwilling to perish"

even the slave under the whip,
even the soldier moaning on the field,
even the prisoner in an iron cage,
even the wife manacled to a brute,
even the mother watching her child starve,
even the child chained in a factory,
even these prefer existing
to its alternative, so benevolent
is creation,
so sublime the
city

II.28

do we love love
or merely its
footprints? do we speak
of a city, or does
the city speak for us?

& those who were "never
apostate," who never
waivered, never

questioned their order,
does the city
speak for them?

11.29

I, apostate, unlikely
christ, worked in a city &
beheld the holy trinity—
boss-man, worker, secretary—
in my heyday I
slept with the secretary,
procured for the boss,
drank with the worker,
left nothing
to imagination
and yet the image
stood before me:
the waif
the amputee
the addict
the beggar,
manwoman
leaning on
its stick

11.30

"six is a perfect number" because
two crutches and
one leg plus the holy
trinity equal it, aliquot like
any other human,
city of cells & organs

11.31

I'm seventy-
one today, a prime,
within but not a factor in
this perfect city

11.32

a woman waves to me
from her walker—
can I look at something?
she lives in a two-
story walkup, chair-lift
monopolizing the stair—
her fridge has gone out &
she needs to get a new
one to the second floor
and sears won't do it

she's 89, she tells me

maybe a small crane or
cherry-picker could
get it to the second
floor casement?

it will be costly, she
knows, but she saved
because the old fridge
was covered under the
extended warranty,
so she figures she can
afford the cost,
within reason
of course

her name is sue

11.33

the tent cities
under the interstate
stabilize:
generators appear,
air conditioners,
motor scooters

I see the one-
armed woman
several blocks from her
appointed corner,
huffing down banks street,
unlit cigarette still
protruding

"the creation is presented in sum,
and then its parts are enumerated..."

11.34

"the head is the seat
of the phlegm"
thinks the city
in the depths of
its gyri and sulci,
chthonic folds
where the divine light
of reason
imagines itself

12.00

ah if only alaric
had finished the job
and not settled
for a few crates of jewels
and some quick pussy,
had he gone ahead &
overwritten the scrolls,
burned the libraries and
those haunted cloisters,
what millennia of
spiritual angst
and prison architecture
he could have saved us—
imagine the golden

tower that might
have been erected
in place of the courthouse,
inscription in... well...
god knows...
not latin...

12.01

a scientific analysis of
the behavior of angels
reveals that half do
as they please and half
as pleases me—which
half is falling into darkness
and which into shining light
remains to be seen

12.02

"no nature is contrary save
that which does not exist"
so that would be me,
the most contrary of folk,
with about as much
essentia as a feather
floating down
from a hawk-ruined nest,
nothing
but a disturbance in the air
where something in-
visible just passed by

12.03

augustine claims
nature is always good and
vice, resistance to nature,
always evil

his sole
responsibility:
to be true to
his own desire

12.04

"it is ridiculous to condemn
the faults of beasts and trees"
and indeed of augustine
who snarls and bites
just as sharply, whose
sap rises just as surely,
rough bark and
dried-out leaves, mangy
fur and leg hiked up,
all those failings which
were bleached away
when plato said 'tree' &
'dog,' (it does assist
a philosopher to have
a nice garden and
clever gardeners
to tend it)

12.05

"that which was made
of nothing," manwoman,
for example, which created
itself from nothing,
nothing from nothing
language of nothings
sweet nothings of the
language suite

12.06

for the city
is not the buildings
but the voids between them

not the people
but the voids between them

not the words
but the spaces between

the beggar
reaches through
my window
into the void

the lawyer
opens a book
into the void

the coroner opens
a case

not the words but
the space between

12.07

the city
is most efficient
when most deficient,
most effective
when most defective

it is actually not
what it factually is

as we see darkness,
as we hear silence,
we live in the city

12.08

essentially, then, the city
is made of nothing

nothing drives the cranes,
nothing pours the concrete

it isn't that it's evil
and has emptied out

it isn't that anyone
has defected to fields
of golden daffodils

but that a defect can
be thought, a field
imagined—

for the city is a field
of thought and image

12.09

certain structures
collapse, certain
structures are
shored up

it's like a metaverse
that keeps happening
when you take
off the headset

and anything goes:
darth vader wins,
luke actually gets
to fuck his sister

12.10

anyone who thinks
the city is as
old as it seems
was born yesterday

and borne across
into the language

12.11

there may be planets ga-
lore, "numberless" cont-
ingencies, effects that
render the most rigorous
observations suspect,
still we insist on a sky
of pure cyan, an hor-
izon of pink flame

12.12

how could anyone
so young conceive
an existence beyond
yesterday? it's tough to
conceive a history when
you personally have none, or then
again maybe the younger
the better, the more gullible
the better

12.13

to prove the path
is straight and narrow
is a circuitous journey

12.14

it's difficult for us–who
imagine the earth as
an ancient mother and
god as a wise old man–
to conceive that it was all
created yesterday, yet
scripture from moses
to foucault con-
clusively proves
this is the case

12.15

before god
created time
it was and will be
difficult to imagine
before and after–
& were there little
angels running
around back then?
or was the play-
ground empty but
for the slides and
swings? and maybe a
poor, lost, confused little
rat terrier searching for
its vanished lord and
master

12.16

& when, exactly,
did god create
eternity?

12.17

before the first
there were none at all,
nor after,
emptiness coeternal
with the sempiternal,
semi-eternal manwoman
lost in its language,
in the trance
of its drumbeat

12.18

"the very hairs
of your head
are numbered"
says the christ
channeling
jeremy bentham,
grace in the panopticon,
sweet assurance of
eternal surveillance

12.19

jules

she walks in
gutterpunk regalia,
dirt tan dimming
the tattoos, rings
in ears nose mouth,
calf-high boots pain-
stakingly laced,
and a possum,
teeth bared,
riding on her shoulder—
an odor, pungent
and comforting as

a stable, hangs
in the air when she
passes, under the sagging
oaks and balconies of the
ancient city

12.20

augustine and
nietzsche square
off on the notion of
periodic revolution
(they obviously
didn't know covid),
one crying sacrilege &
the other pumping his
fist saying 'yes let's
sack religion
once and for all'

then someone
changes the subject,
a world shifts
its focus, and they
go on arguing
inside their jar

12.21

god made the single
man then reached in and jerked
out a rib and started licking it

'whoa, man,'
god sd., 'this is yum!'

so we all have the same
granddad, all descended
from that same bone, that's

why we all
love each other
so much

12.22

covid returns

this morning, again, that
feeling of broken glass
in the throat,
shaking with
fever so bad I
can't open
the ibuprofen–
how parkinson's
must feel–
I saw it coming
when I bought
a ticket to the
poetry festival in sant-
iago, ill-fated
pilgrimage

12.23

was god, who made
us "in his own image"
also wracked with
fever? with that broken
glass in his throat?
is that what made
it so hard to speak?
in the beginning was
the broken glass,
tearing god's throat,
the broken image

12.24

in *dei* daze
citizens stroll
elbows linked,
pointillist tranquility
of the lockstep mind,
skirting the voids until
they wake in the gutter
and head
to the cathedral
for a fix

12.25

which came first, the
chicken or eternity?
god or the god's
delirium?

the mother
who was a foetus
now carries a foetus,
the old man
who could not rest
now
confined to his bed

that body, "which is
not itself constructed"
negotiates with
god for
renovation, an up-
grade, & god's got
just the thing

12.26

body is housing
for the way-
ward soul—

cities cellblocks,
subdivisions,
wards & precincts,
some for rent, some
ripe for squatting

12.27

that single man
adam
silhouette in the set-
ting son, like the
closing credits of
road warrior, wo-
manless and ribless,
solitary, muscular,
figurine inside
the monk's hood,
muttering to himself,
absorbed in naming

13.00

images of prison,
of the carceral body,
prefigure the notion
"that death is penal,"
we're locked inside the
body like the bad
ass in solitary—
guards and trustees
pass by and fuck
with you all day long

13.01

madam I'm adam–
manwoman created in
rhetorical flourish, in its
own (mirror) image

able was elba
also, conquerors
brought low by
rising inflection

13.02

everyone knows
about the death of the body
when the soul leaves the
animal carcass behind
and trails toward eternity,
but we seldom speak
of that "second death"
which, for christians,
occurs when, after death,
the corporeal resurrection they
banked their eternal souls on
doesn't happen, and they
die in their sleep

13.03

"he suffered in his members
the warring of disobedient
lust," remarks the saint on
that first man, who thus infected
eve who passed it on, like
syphilis, to the unsuspecting un-
born, who then had to be
remanded to the house of
correction (i.e. the body) until such
time as the triumvirate pass
sentence (in their laborious
syntax), sending
sinners into the furnace and
good boys and girls to an
eternal bouncy castle

13.04

'is this free?'
she says
of my five-spot
as she grabs it
through the window,
unlit cigarette still
dangling from her lips–
'what do you mean?'
I say–
'free money?'
she says–
it's thanksgiving
season, recently
turned cold, and
she has on a nice
new jacket of
white fleece,
empty sleeve tucked
into a pocket
concealing the
missing arm–
she doesn't mention
jesus today

13.05

what the law is to
the criminal,
death is
to the saint

for as the wicked
live poorly
"the good
die well"

13.06

when the covid finally
lifts it leaves behind
a guilty residue
in the soul that mirrors
the green snot in the
body

through what omission
comes this emission?
neither through kissing
nor pissing
have I sullied my
self, nor through
indiscretion of the hands,
which leaves only
language to blame,
my over-attention, my leaning
(as my hearing wanes)
into the viral mist that goes
before the impassioned words of
prophets and singers, my
politeness in the face of
the raving drunk, my
reluctance to shirk the
rancid breath of a friend

likewise nations
infect each other
speaking

which makes me wonder if
even gods, so famously
wed to the word,
are immune

13.07

fifa world cup in qatar

muhammed, on the other
hand, prescribes language
through the mask, which filters
95% of talk about
slave camps
and the proleptic houris (i.e.
whores) that service
the better hotel rooms

thus the fifa pres
(who moved there)
can enjoy from his pent-
house the stunning view
of the man-made
islands and del-
iciously guilty
pregame pleasures
with no fear of discovery

13.08

augustine's saints may be spared the
"second death," but
the new orleans saints
seem to merit one
every game

in fulfillment of the
prophecy, fans dress up in
pope gear and gyrate
and pray, but it does
no good, no one, nothing
intercedes

13.09

should we be calling
the living living
when they are in fact dying,
and the dying dying
when they are yet living?

why, pray adam,
are we calling
anything anything?
why are
we calling?

calling and calling

13.10

seneca cynically
trudged toward death
and got there
as surely as
any saint—he
covered a lot
of ground (and
papyrus) along the way
that followers still follow
to this day

13.11

"let us, then, speak
in the customary way,—
no man ought to speak otherwise"
(for death, strictly
declined, whether noun
verb, gerund or part-
iciple, is just death
as we customarily say)

13.12

'everybody wants to get to
heaven but nobody wants
to die,' carpenters say, citing
augustine, at least in spirit, in-
spiring the crew to
the demands of capital, for just
as living is dying and
everything is nothing,
no one is anyone
without quotation

13.13

membership:

PIE mems-ro, *from* mems- *'flesh, meat,'*
sanskrit mamsam *'flesh,'*
greek meninx *'membrane,'*
mēros *'thigh,' gothic* mimz *'flesh,'*
in common use, 'one of the
limbs or extremities,' especially 'the
sex organ,' latin membrum virile,
originally of women as well as men,
'a christian,' a 'member' of the
church, the 'body of christ'

fig leaf as first
figuration, disavowal,
displacement by which
"they experienced a new motion
of their flesh," adam's
hardon beating
the bush, leaves
trembling

13.14

embrace your vice
is lacan's advice—
vitiate your member
augustine's

see if you can coax
from your "corrupt root"
that second death
which is the second coming

for "the author of natures
created man upright...
of his own will corrupted
and justly condemned..."

13.15

25 november, 2022 (black friday)

these overcast days, neither hot
nor cold, sunless but dry,
with a slight electric
charge in the air,
remind me of home,
that study in brown and gray
that was my youth

home it was—every
morning the wind
lifting the curtain
on the same drab walls—
yet always with the feeling
I'd soon be packing up
and leaving for home, some
other home, someplace I
had never been but was
more home than this

now half a cent-
ury into the new,
still anticipating,
like I might be heading
back most any day now, drift-
ing off every night thinking
tomorrow might be the one

13.16

ah you poor
deluded fucks who (like
plato) still believe
separation of body and
soul is not penal—
the shadow-life
you lead is of
your own choosing

13.17

"...the earth, which is the central
member in the body of a greater
creature..."

world as
god's phallus

every color every
shape every room
every window every sen-
sation

being as
coming

every sidewalk every
flower every
bright spring day

13.18

why are you still
here, in this
corner of a city
most have forgotten?

I'm dreaming
your dreams for you

why do you still
stand in mute
defiance? what
is there to oppose?

I'm seeing
your world for you

what do you
want? do you beg only
for something
to beg for?

I'm living
your life for you

parasite!
I'll drink this
poison
to be rid of you

13.19

should I regret that
my life has afforded
me insufficient pleasure
in the past?
or dread that
there will be even
less going forward?—

nostalgia for the life
I didn't live
as well as for the one
I did?

paradox
of time and
sensation

13.20

for the first couple
had neither time
nor sensation (even as
good-looking as they
surely were) but lusted
only after knowledge

later, literate but
spent, they smoked
cigarettes in the afterglow,
did the crossword puzzle,
imagined a
city someone might
someday conceive and
its sojourn
across the earth

13.21

"thus paradise is the church...
the four rivers the four gospels...
the fruit-trees the saints...
the tree of life is the holy of holies, christ...
the tree of knowledge the will's free choice"

everything is something
else, circular, language
woven into itself

seamless
like a shroud

13.22

"the bodies of the righteous [i.e. angels]
such as they shall be in the resurrection"
will resemble the bodies of
rich people, in that they will eat
not to stave off hunger but merely
to be social with their less
well-heeled, merely human, friends

augustine is silent, however,
on the matter
of defecation

will the angels also engage in
mystical shitting, sitting
with us in the next stall &
making poot noises
on their arm
just so we feel at home?

13.23

there is much to be said
(in the interest of scientific clarification)
of the animal body vs. the
spiritual body and the subtle differences
between spirit and soul and
earth and flesh, most especially when,
insensate, the earthy meat
rejoins its medium (in whatever state
of disrepair) while the
spiritual body heads off to a banquet
at god's right hand

13.24

whether we under-
stand breathing
as the intaking
of the holy breath
or the out-
blowing of colorful
spirits, whether
as aspiration or
inspiration,
inflation of the soul
or deflation of
the spirit,
how co2 and
tobacco fit
into god's plan
remains as mysterious
as the "concupiscence
in the unruly members
of our first parents"
whose means and
methods we must now
examine:

14.00

sunday morning,
vape pen on this
clear december day,
pain-free, randy but lazy,
lazy and broken,
obits & word games &
last night's regret

this wound I don't remember
receiving, was it in the garden
or in the city? will discovering
the origin heal it, or is that
only a habit of speaking?

as a child I ran naked
in the edenic woods,
basking in shame like a
dog rolling in the leaves,
smoking among the leaves

speaking is a habit
compared to which
smoking is child's play

14.01

we say "by the grace
of god" meaning
sheer luck,
narrowest chance,
by the grace of
nothing

nothing sent
into adam
the second death

nothing cast them
out of the garden

in the beginning was
the word, and the word
was nothing

14.02

a styrofoam cup
appears in my window
while I'm stopped at the
light at claiborne & esplanade

at first it seems
to levitate, then I

notice the stick
it is impaled upon

a crepe myrtle branch
growing from the hand
of an old man seated
in his walker on the curb

when he catches my eye
he bounces the limb
enticingly, but the light changes
and I drive on

14.03

"the father of lies"
has many children, like
that poor dad
in the tent city,
under the freeway

14.04

god's truth,
says paul the pol
(to the romans, iii 7),
speaks through my lie

thus the apostle
prefigures his descendants,
who accidentally confess
their own sins in their
accusations of others,
trump blowing the whistle
on fraudulent elections,
for example, or
augustine on erections

14.05

my grandson tears
apart a safety razor
and cuts himself
as his uncle used to,
track of incisions,
stair-steps down the arm

what original sin,
what guilty infection,
transmitted through
father after father,
fathered this,
our misshapen identity?

quiet in the house,
the day spent lounging,
long night of counseling
and stitches recompensed
by suspension of
work and school

local news muted
on the flickering tv,
strip of white
gauze showing at
his wrist, just below
the gray flannel cuff

14.06

"of the human will":
the evil live
by vice, he says, volition
of consent, and not
by nature, while volition
of aversion makes desire
vile, volition of joy
inspires the will to death,

volition of fear, the
turning away from that
which is too horrible to face,
volition of sorrow, when that
which was greatly feared
has come to pass

14.07

love evolves, apparently,
in voluntary submission,
waxes then wanes
with the language,
diligent, amorous, char-
itable

augustine takes pains
(having aged
past caring, perhaps)
to strike-through
difference, to level
love to a universal
synonymy, a beginning
word, and in this
way truly does
anticipate the hippies...

so maybe dylan's
sappy version
in a sappy way
got it right

14.08

"these precise proprieties of
language" give way to e-
quivalent appropriations in
the soul, itself
conjured in the matrix
of meanings

language feeling
the force of the will
it created

14.09

"...they grieve because they themselves groan
within themselves, waiting for the adoption,
the redemption of their body..."

today I happened to pass
by the old house and saw
your deadname & your
sister's name written
in the concrete sidewalk

I guess
you were out there
or your parents were
when the city poured it

perturbations
of the past:
both the memory
and the forgetting
are homage

"rather a verbal than a
real dispute" says
augustine, as if the
name might settle in-
to the soul's state,
fluid gradually
turning to stone

14.10

if we were blessed
from the beginning

how describe the longing
for bliss
here in the trans-
itory world,
unless the longing
were the blessing,
the bliss the wishing?

what the city
announces from
every pothole
and manhole, from
every concrete truck
pouring its liquid
into the form

14.11

"he chose the serpent
as his mouthpiece"
because the wending &
twisting of its body resembled
language

he chose the tree
to be entwined in
because it reminded him of the crooked
streets of the medina

and he chose the woman
to tempt because he was
so tempted

14.12

on jan. 2 we walk the tent
city with cabbage and black-
eyed peas, handing out plates

a circle of men sitting on broken
chairs and buckets in a hollow
in the garbage

what you can't see driving
by: the smell of piss and
delicacies of attitude, haughty

the crappy chocolate muffins
someone picked up at the grocery
on their way over, are far

more popular than the home-
cooked veggies, taken
without a word

14.13

"it is useful," augustine says,
"for the proud to fall into an open and in-
disputable transgression, and so
displease themselves, as already, by
pleasing themselves, they had fallen"

is it gravity that draws
this ink through the quill?
or only the vacuum
of the empty page?
or is there a river of ink
it wants to flow into?

'spontaneous' figures,
working without
a net, without
the solace
of erasure

words wrap around
the body of christ,
a soft blanket

14.14

I am proud
to have been with you

my you, my
second person,
the one I cannot
not name, sacred
symbol you,
sacral one
I sin with

14.15

"as when one breaks a pen, or
crushes a quill that writes badly"

the house, inherited, was allowed
to deteriorate, holes in the roof
allayed with buckets,
or with nothing,
blankets on the floor,
or nothing

dan had caught a whiff of
something dead
in the backyard a few
days ago, but the crowd of
cops and coroner's helpers
that showed up with blue
lights flashing today caught him
unawares

one young man, interviewed
on channel six, stopped,
just a few days ago,
on his way to the store
and talked to mister alonzo
on his front porch, and then,

on the way back
stopped and talked
for a few minutes more

14.16

augustine laments (or perhaps
confesses) that the
phallus cannot be "actuated by
volition, in the same way as other
members," but rises of its own
accord, in disregard or even
despite of the will of its owner,
and with this sentiment I
can agree, for as the bishop
wishes he could will the
unruly member to gentle
servitude, I lament it
so reluctant to sin

14.17

you know those dreams
where you are going to the store
or walking into a classroom or
standing up to give a poetry
reading and suddenly realize
you are naked? that's how
it must have been for our
first parents when they woke and
set to sewing fig leaves,
all thumbs,
nervous gymnosophists

14.18

23-01-07

"lust requires for its consummation
darkness and secrecy," like kevin
mccarthy, in the back alley before

the fifteenth vote, where no
doubt a bit of metaphysical
fellatio did come into play

for to love power is
to love one's self
alone
in the dark

14.19

I see the one-armed
beggar walking back to
canal street from behind
the cemetery on banks

she stomps, waving her
one arm and rotating
the stump, mouth moving
in an angry soliloquy

as I pass by she
points the nub at me
like some kind of gun
then leans her head,
sticks out her tongue,
and licks it

14.20

diogenes the cynic
(or "canine")
copulated with his wife in
public (indeed
like a dog), though augustine
believes this was only a
"pretence of copulation,"
like modern pornstars
the cheery couple
merely mimed desire

for the audience,
for the desire is
for the audience,
why they mimed,
why mimes mime

14.21

"they
understand by the earth
the body"
which my grandson
plows with their
razor,
planting a pronoun
to harvest a name

14.22

"two sexes manifestly distinct,"
argues the saint

when I was 10 my cousin
taught me the distinction
between male and female
bolt threads and blushed
when he said it, covering with
a snicker

fashionista vs. piss-smelling derelict,
gourmet vs. dumpster diver,
chauffeur-driven vs. bicycle trailer…
the city is heir to this shame

14.23

"we command our bodily members
as children… but the vicious parts
must be treated as slaves"

if the city treats its members
as the body its, then these
beggars and addicts are the gen-
italia, to be fondled and flogged
until they yield up their pleasure/
pain to the social body and
the city comes

lying filth in the capitol
(santos, for example)
lie in the filth of their
infrastructures, sleep under
the bridges they
appropriate

"the field of generation
should have been sown
by the organ created for
this purpose"

14.24

"for we move at will not only those members
which are furnished with joints of solid bone,
as the hands, feet, and fingers, but we move
also at will those which are composed of slack
and soft nerves: we can put them in motion, or
stretch them out, or bend and twist them, or
contract and stiffen them"

politics, democracy begins
in the body, demo-
cracy among
the members,
outward and
inward flow, ebb
which brings forth
language

14.25

"he wishes to live,
he is compelled to die"
(and this applies as well
to the one who compels)

self-command
overflows the body
seeps into the city
wicking up the skyscrapers
floor by floor

14.26

"modesty shuts my mouth, although
my mind conceives the matter clearly,"
dods himself might have said, as
he leaves untranslated the passage
in which augustine describes the physi-
ognomy of our first father, who was
able to insert his member, without ardor, inside
first mother and "inject" the reproductive force
without disrupting the hymen
(perhaps the added friction even
enhanced the experience?)
as the english flows around
this page of virginal latin

14.27

that certain knowledge
be forgot and we (again,
as before the fall?) know
without knowing, act
without acting

here where identities end or
trailing end of an identity

poet on the verge of a
death more final than
deaths that have gone before,
a second death, or
even a third

our creation which
challenges us to a duel

I pass beneath the cypress trees
I lie down in the field
I talk like the crows talk

the slightest touch bruises me

14.28

"two cities have been formed
by two loves:"
both *amor*, ("*amor
sui*," "*amor dei*")

not *diligere*
not *caritas*

love of being being
love of non-being

crowd of stars
spreading across
this rhetorical universe

15.00

mardi gras 2023

china sends up a cele-
bratory balloon which biden
gaily pops with a pin

earth moves, god
seems restless, cities
which war has not yet toppled
fall in upon themselves,
citizens piled
among the rubble

fat tuesday approaches,
last theoretical blast of
debauchery before
the atonement of lent

blue lights flashing
at the tent city under
the freeway:
make way for
the parades

make way for
paradise

15.01

"these we also mystically
call the two cities"

network
of antitheses,
propensities that almost
cancel

& the one
victorious
is the one
appearing to lose

until the polarities
collapse and we are
"grafted into christ"

15.02

jerusalem fore-
shadows the possibility
of a city, one part
slummy, populated by
bond women, one part
golden, decorated
by bourgeois wives,
"sarah, the free woman,
who prefigured the free city"—
indeed gave birth
to it like isaac—
sends the concubine's
bastard packing
in a pauline parable
that illustrates beautifully paul's
problem with parables,
as both the vessel of
wrath and the vessel of
mercy spill their
libations in the end

15.03

of tribes wandering
the desert is the city born,
old clan divisions, blood
feuds and cousins'
marriage, con-
cretized in these
walls and alleys

perambulations of
law, codes of
conduct, ownership
in the abstract,
or just the *jus
imperium* of the
scorpion squad

illicit loves
spawning ex-
plicit murders

the obvious solidarity
never the true one

15.04

sex after the promenade
on mardi gras day

walking the dog
in the quiet evening—
the city I am in
seems as far away
as the faint noise of the
conflagration still
raging in the quarter

the dog sniffs and
licks at the crevices
and corners of
my city my hometown

15.05

romulus slew remus as
cain abel, so that each
could claim to have founded
a city, one earthly,
the other moreso,
"the carnal lusts
of two men"
lie in this dust

15.06

"'let not the sun go
down upon your wrath,'"

augustine quotes
(paul, ostensibly,
addressing heraclitus),
a tall order if you live in
donbas or syria or
uvalde or most
any place really, as putin
slips on his fur coat
(sable, exquisite)
for a winter no
sun will set upon

15.07

so god had words
with cain, in that easy
conversational tone he
used with the first fam,
but this little chat
needs laborious interpretation
for these idle remarks contain
(albeit in obscure form) the
first documentations of that
city of junkies and slumlords
cain founded, like *mahagonny*,
in spite when god snubbed his
offering

of the "turning" (*conuersio*,
in dods's view, no doubt a
casualty of the septuagint scandal [q.v.],
since the hebrew appears
to render 'desire')
augustine provides an
exhaustive analysis
that does not mention
a change in seasons

15.08

it seems unlikely
that cain would build a city
when there were only
four people (and soon to be
three) on the planet to
inhabit it, perhaps
cain as well as
augustine shored up his
language with conjecture,
puppets and effigies and
silhouettes in the
windows

15.09

augustine, homer and pliny
all lament
that the human race seems
to be growing smaller in stature
and shorter in life-span
as the centuries pass

adam, enoch, methuselah
all lived hundreds of years,
and those huge
bones and that great
tooth augustine saw
on the shore at utica
reveal that the ancients were
giants
compared to us

and how history
has borne out
the poets' concern,
as today we seem
to have shrunk
to tiny ants

crawling around
an apple,
and live
but a day

15.10

enoch, "translated
without death,"
apparently got into heaven
without having to die

there also appear
discrepancies in calculation
(did adam beget seth at age
230 or 130? did he live 700
or 800 years longer?) between
the "hebrew originals" and "our
manuscripts," which point to
the fallibility (as all things human)
of translation (which dods
does little to allay)

which leads
me to wonder if that enoch
who appeared in paradise
was precisely the same
enoch who sired methuselah
on earth
or if some nuance
or idio-
matic subtlety of the real
live historical figure might
have been lost in the process

and those of us who did
not please god and will
be translated in the
normal, moldering
way? what will we

signify or imply
in that foreign
tongue of paradise?

15.11

"...it is not credible
that the seventy
translators
who simultaneously and unanimously
produced one
rendering, could
have erred, or,
in a case
in which no
interest of theirs was involved,
could have falsified
their translation;
but that the jews,
envying us
our translation of
their law and prophets,
have made alterations in their texts
to undermine the
authority of ours."

& perhaps the catholics,
envying us english
our translation of augustine,
changed the latin to likewise
discredit dods's conversion of
conuersio

15.12

at 3 a.m.
in this city of
anxious dreams
a muscle
spasm in my neck

makes me yelp like
a puppy
and wake my-
self, & I lie
in the dark as
faces from the
past file by,
searching for their names

15.13

it is likely we owe
our confusion
"neither to the malice of the jews
nor to men so diligent and prudent
as the seventy translators,
but to the error of the copyist..."

perhaps, even, to augustine's
own amanuensis...
& how many scribes,
how many
translators since?

15.14

for his six
hundredth birthday god
gave noah his
flood and a promise
he'd make the latin
translators pay
closer attention to the hebrew
in the future and be more
careful with their math besides,
and after two short
millennia he'd give us
google translate and
the atomic clock, &
auto-correct which virtually

eliminates transcription
errors in the celestial city

15.15

is it conceivable that any
red-blooded healthy male
with an ernest
desire to populate a
city with his progeny and
attended by faith-
ful wives & concubines
could live a century or more
without impregnating
one or two along the way?
the answer to this text-
ual mystery is simply that
only sons of royal lineage
are worthy of mention, the good
book having not time to record
every bastard son
every fallen daughter
spawned by the patriarch

15.16

"the sexual intercourse of man and woman...
is in the case of mortals
a seed-bed of the city..."

that city which "sojourns"
from the bridal bower
to the whore's corner
in its midnight crawl

15.17

the etymology of "adam" is a gender-
reveal without ultrasound, an answer
for which no question was posed

adam splits by meiosis into
twin cities, one with an unspoken deadname
one unnamed for all eternity

& these cities sojourn
across the earth
from rome to annaba
from the boot to the capere
from the horn to good hope
to gibraltar, to kharkiv, to santa cruz

15.18

the dog and I
walking in the woods

at city
park

leaves crackle under my
boots like insects on a slab

typing with two thumbs
on a smart phone

this ode to dying
in a dying art

15.19

"...but this is that man
who was translated..."

I try to focus
on the phallus, but
my gaze wanders
from the page, seeks out
the dream someone next
door is having

in dreams we are indiscrete
like this,
but in bodies
defined by
a membrane, the
skin,
god's condom,
the touch
without touching

15.20

"...the pedigree of christ...
and to what terminus...?"

cascade of
generations from christ's
member, the in-
terminable succession

when I was in grade
school, the pastor once based
his sermon on the long chain
of begats; afterwards my
father complained the
idiot had talked for
a solid hour about
absolutely nothing

15.21

"...scripture begins
to reckon the times..."

jus imperium in-
herits the word

the right of writing
goes without saying

while the rite of writing
is a movement of the lips

like prayer
like telling the rosary

slave merchants and clerics, those
who keep the records

15.22

so the sons of god were
tempted (and sorely) by
the daughters of men
and wived them noisily

it sounded like two cities
crashing together
while sojourning
across the earth

& they fell in love
but they didn't fall
in love with love

they begat sons &
they begat daughters &
their sons & their daughters
didn't fall in love
with love either

they fell in love with war

it sounded like two cities
crashing together

15.23

when a breeze blows across
the body of a woman

fauns and angels contemplate
spawning a race of giants

but the angel is only
a messenger
and its sperm only
the ink on a missive

one day the love child
outgrows its mother's house
one day it leaves footprints
cars could fall into

15.24

beginning of april, 2023

outside greenwood cemetery,
beneath the bronze stag that tops
the elk's lodge mausoleum,
the one-armed beggar
leans against the iron
fence in a new spring dress,
cigarette dangling, card-
board sign tucked illegibly
under the stump

behind her, the confederate
monument (600 bodies beneath
the mound, they say),
the gothic cupola of the
firemen's association, and the more
efficient, doric, crypt dedicated
to the fraternal order of police

down on claiborne they
are scooping up tents
and belongings—shirtless
men argue

with the front-end loader
or simply watch

the lieutenant
governor is
proposing a fence
painted with
mardi gras floats
to surround the encampment,
& inside installing 'a couple
of portable toilets'

15.25

just as god pretends
to be angry in the midst of his
"unchangeable tranquility"
so that dull humans can
understand his motive as he
floods the world, overtopping
levees, swamping crypts,
mansions and tent cities alike,
so lt. gov. nungesser puffs
up his impatience with the un-
washed rabble when
in reality he could give
a shit about this
stinking, sinking
last-ditch effort of a
city

15.26

and just as the church rep-
resents two kinds of
men (cut and uncut), the three
storeys of the ark
stand for the three
branches of government
(executive, legislative, and extra-

judicial) who cry out to fema
when the levee gives way
and three
chord blues
comes to stay

15.27

I'm stopped at the red light &
she comes to the window

up close the arm
is more mangled than it appears
from afar, cords of scar tissue,
tracks of whatever machine did
it, back then

she wears a black scarf over
her hair like
an hajib or simple habit

when I hand her
two dollars
she says:

thank you I'm sister
sarah I mean I'm sister jean
at night I have to wear
a chastity belt
because of the incest
because they tricked me and
took my sons away
they told me he was a distant
cousin but it was actually in-
cest and they took my sons
away I have two sons 18
and 12 they tricked me
you see
they told me he was a distant
cousin so I have to

*wear a chastity belt
but now I'm going to
trick them
I don't want any more sons
pray for me*

as I pull away I watch
in the mirror as
she crosses
to a parked car, then takes
a key from her
pocket and opens it

16.00

dave

these past days together
in this house remind
me that the city is based
on everyone having
a cell to go home to

a tribe has no cells
an island has no cells
under the interstate
there are no cells

the bee has cells
where it stores
its nectar

16.01

"...the planting of the vine by noah,
and his intoxication by its fruit,
and his nakedness while he slept...
are all of them pregnant with
prophetic meanings,
and veiled in mysteries"

a text which has been translated
directly to the city of god
and saved the
ignominy of death...

had augustine's employer not
hidden the holy
script in its basement for that
fateful millennium
writing would have a different
aura today,
which is to say
the city makes concrete
from the dust of its ancestors

16.02

shem and japheth
(mr. cut and mr. uncut)
entered the room back-
wards so as not to have to see
daddy noah's winkie
sticking up in his sleep

"their backs" says augustine,
"signify the memory of things
past," so we can forget
the phallus by
focusing on it,
foreshadowing
frenchmen street &
festival season, the real
meaning of justice's
blindfold

so please
pass the wine—
blood of the vine,

seed of the house
of israel—let's
get drunk and fuck

16.03

upon this body
politic, a severely infected
sebaceous cyst,
antibiotics suppressing
'voter fraud' until
surgery can be scheduled

hydromorphone and fentanyl
help the pained
city sleep
while the courts uphold
the gerrymandered
white count

16.04

as "the tongue is
the instrument of domination"
the giant nimrod
slimed together a tower that
looked exactly like his
dick from a distance
and with honeyed
words attempted to lure some
houris to come lick it,
but as he lay down
the lovely voices of
babylon turned
to babble in his ear
and the sword
leapt into his hand

16.05

let's pretend (since he's

already everywhere)
god came down
to confound
our speech,
gurgled mellifluously &
no one
could remember
what duck meant
or line

16.06

the royal we
plus me
make three
& this holy trinity
spoke to the angels
on our behalf
(so to speak)
in 72 actually
73 languages
but kept it simple
down south, where
"...we know several
barbarous nations
which have but one language"

16.07

who brought these
beasts to the islands
after the flood?
did they emerge from
the earth across
vast seas and fuck
like bunnies till
things got going
again? ah the many
mysteries that arise when a
language imagines itself

16.08

monstrous tribes
of monstrous men
mixed in among
the seraphim—
what do we call
trump? what
tucker carlson?
what that one
with the single leg
shielding eyes from the sun
with its foot?
hermaphrodites &
hermaphroditesses make
their way unwitting
into a discourse
on siamese twins, hyper-
textual pickled
punks, still—
descendents of adam,
descendents of noah,
survivors

16.09

a light mist blurs the morning
on this day in late april, 2023, fest-
ival season around here
at the bottom of the map

seasons, decades go by
sitting at red lights
glancing uncomfortably
at the beggars on the curb

everything I have been
taught to desire I
no longer desire

everything I
have wished away I
now want to keep

body fails, starts to fester,
long before its reason ceases &
long before it loses its
sense of smell

16.10

the only things
to talk about are
the words we
talk about them
with, what the slip,
the um, the double-
back, the sigh,
the sneeze and
the stutter mean—
for the etymology of
babble is not babel,
though its history
is

16.11

first father of figuration
takes word and world
quite literally, &
what we call
metaphors, god's
misprision

16.12

"in the deluge of superstition
that floods the whole world"
we have only this text for ark—

midrash suggests
scripture does not exist
until it has
been scripted

a u might
carry water, for example,
to slake a traveler's thirst

a v can hold flowers
and be a shrine
to honor our ancestors

even the venom
in the fangs of the s
can be put to good use

16.13

remember too that
the sargassum island
sojourns
off the shore of
florida,
mystically influencing desantis
to reinstall aug-
ustinian orthodoxy
in sarasota, and the new
pres at new college says
he'll unfund critical
race theory and put
those woke motherfuckers
to sleep for good

here city of god meets
city of an other
and the broken husks
wash up on shore…
the stench follows you
for miles down the beach

16.14

I was a country rube
come to the city
from the arkansas woods
bee trees and whitewashed shacks

name of my city:
city of no-god

I was already
75 when I moved here
205 years ago

now my ears ring
and my vision is poor
and I imagine leaving
this city, one day

I imagine wandering
across a desert
or maybe across a sea
like the sea of galilee

on its shore is another city
the city of no-man
with winding streets
stone stairways &
terraces the color of stars

16.15

cleaning my fingernails
in church, beneath
the drone of a church
father, phantasies on
the hard pews,
church lady
hiking up her dress
to pee, pointilist vision through

hammered glass,
my signature in
semen in the hymnal

16.16

small dis-
crepancies in a-
braham's timetable
needn't detract
from infallible
scribbles,
goatskin scrolls
rolled and stowed and
strapped onto an ass
who carried it,
with that sad
resigned
demeanor all
donkeys seem
to have,
all the way
to new orleans

16.17

"...rome, as it were
another babylon
in the west..."
where the tower
of latin aimed
death rays
at the vulgar
till god made
the world trade center
and no one could
understand anything
anymore

16.18

precious text
my lovely sol-
iloquy,
how I love
to fiddle
with you

you're perfect,
tightly woven
fabric, like
a sieve
for knowing things,
bindle of facts

even a day
like this,
wasted in dumb
euphoria, lying
in the park,
in the faint
hum of a transformer,
will catch something

I lie
in the grass
among flowers and flax
& leave an impression
like a sleeping
deer

maybe a sensitive
nose like my
dog's will detect:
something living
lay here

16.19

& the pharaoh took
abram's sister-wife
sarai to be his own
lawfully wedded, but gave
her back when he got
too sick to enjoy

she remained chaste
through the whole thing
or at least mystically so
as augustine decis-
ively proved in his contra to
faustus the manichæan,
killing two birds
to preserve one hymen

16.20

when lot got rich e-
nough he needed
to get away from over-
bearing uncle abram
and besides feeling
certain urges
threw his lot
in with the sodomites and
headed across the sahara
with his concubines and
camels, sort of like desantis to-
day struggling to get
trump's avuncular
dick out of his ass and start
his own orgy in iowa (with
casey behind him all
the way of course)

16.21

"...that figure the greeks
call hyperbole..."

and abraham's offspring (i.e. us)
shall cover the earth like
dust, god said,
like the sand of the sahara

if you can count the grains
of the sahara
you can count your heirs,
is what god said

slight exaggeration, perhaps,
but god was making a point

16.22

I had thought she had left town,
haven't seen her in weeks until
today, in a newish sundress,
sign again
tucked under the stump,
face set in work-a-day concentration,
cigarette still unlit

and I start to wonder
as I drive to work
this lazy day
in late may
what it will be like
for her in heaven

at the body's resurrection
will the arm return
in jubilant homecoming?
everyone hugging and
dancing in the meadow?

certain now of god's love
she lifts her two arms in
triumph, and then, just to
show off, lights
her cigarette in the wind

16.23

in the next vision god
told abram his offspring would
number as the stars, which raised
augustine's eyebrow since abram
was uncircumcised, and everyone
agreed, back in the day, that even
such a righteous guy as abram
couldn't get into heaven
uncut

16.24

at god's further direction abram
hacked up a heifer, a ram, and a she-
goat, and sat down with
a pigeon and a crow
to enjoy them, but when the
sun went down he got the willies
that the amorites might be
less than lovey-dovey for the next
couple of thousand years
and begged st. augustine to explain
how it was god wasn't just being
a dick here, and lo augustine dreamed
up the concepts of symbol and synecdoche
to cover for god's mendacity,
and referred abram to rhinocorura
where they send liars to fester after
their noses are chopped off, and one
may cower in peace while the
israeli drones pass over

16.25

augustine finds "no wanton lust,
no filthy lewdness" in sarai's
delivery of her handmaid hagar
to her husband, as it was done
"for the sake of progeny... seeking
not guilty excess, but natural fruit,"
though she did, morning after (fig-
uratively speaking), send the little
slut and her bastard son packing,
for the cold (i.e. political) light of day
lends to the rumpled bed a different
hue than the wine-glow of evening,
just like it did for augustine himself
when he kicked his concubine
to the curb—such a long
time ago—what was
her name again?

16.26

failure of vision...

I can no longer read
from a book of standard text
much less a bible

I order new glasses
I adjust the view
on the oversized monitor
so the letters are huge

will I finish
before my eyes do?
or finish blind?

augustine with his quill
and olive oil lamp—
I imagine him in a cloister,

yet surely he lives in luxury
sits at a mahogany desk
in a chair of gilt and velvet,
slaves at either hand

without glasses, at 72, how
does he do it? does he dictate?
or send scratchings to the copyist?

he mentions crushing a quill,
smashing an inkwell—
does he rub his head over his
famous flourishes, the perfect
parallels of his analogies, micro-
scopic perfection of the conceits?

what celestial city awaits
at the end of these
earthly pages

when I crush the quill,
when I throw my meto-
nymic inkwell against the wall

16.27

"born in sin, not
actual but original…"

circumcision, god's covenant
with the "infant,"
renders even the boychild's winkie
phallic by uncovering the crown

and those who are not
the "infant" (i.e. women,
slaves, all manner of
"punic" folk) wait in the wings,
covered but not
in the covenant

16.28

sunday morning, oolong
and oat milk before sunrise
and a tragedy of names,
for upon the revelation of *brit milah*
abram becomes abraham
sarai becomes sarah &
hagar (whom you might
think would become hagara or
something) is forgotten in the holy
uncovering (except one,
one who was never an
"infant" and remained un-
cut, will remember her,
and this is the one who will
set history in motion)

16.29

of the three angel-
men who came
to the oak of mamre
one might have been
christ and two might
have been enough
for abraham (ne abram)
to feel the divine right (vide 3.04)
surging in his loins, for
he had yet sons to bear
(& daughters too, perhaps?)
for the line to finally
trickle down to you

16.30

and lot's wife sighed a
little too longingly for the parties
in sodom and ever after
"furnished to believing men
a condiment" in sexy

silhouette to remind them
of the savor, while abraham
told the king at gerar sarah
was just his sister, go ahead
and have a go, then embarrassed
the entire clan by taking her
back (he'd checked her drawers for
residue, found none!
a miracle!)

16.31

so sarah, because she remained
chaste no matter how many guys
old abraham loosed on her,
shall be the new covenant,
the covenant of the cut, the un-
covering, the velvet crowning,
the city
of god,
while hagar & son,
"sent away," become the other city,
city of tarps and cardboard,
smell of piss and the junkie's stagger,
city of souls barely covered
with ragged flesh, sojourning
to the farthest most barren &
desolatest corner of the earth

16.32

everyone gets excited
about sarah giving birth
at 90 but no one blinks
an eye that abraham
can still get it up at 100, even
in the glade where he
buried her and settled,
the lush spring putting
spring in his step, & lay down

among the grasses, sap
surging in the stem, &
all the world comes
to attention and listens
to the distant thunder,
drones, is it?
headed for beirut

16.33

although maybe this boundless
force did reach a limit
when abraham at 140
told his servant to put her hand
on his old scrotum and swear
like it were a stack of bibles
that she wouldn't be doing the
same to his son's that night

augustine sees in this a
foreshadowing of christ's coming
and indeed of his own, or
so my reading of augustine's
reading of genesis foretells

16.34

of the children of abraham, numerous
as the grains of sand,
sarah's brood (at least
the good-looking ones) jam
the beach at st. augustine, fl.
while hagar's relax at taghazout
on the salty
mare nostrum

the late capitalist
propensity for vacation
empties both cities
of their bourgeois in summer

but these children
of forgotten lineage,
having never registered
a hair sample with
ancestry.com,
still work the corners

16.35

twins doing battle
in rebecca's womb
foretell in hindsight
drones hitting gaza
today, but what accounts
for the ones hitting moscow?

our little
corner of the world,
nostradamus come
to notre dame

16.36

for isaac to fulfill the prophecy
that his seed would number as
the stars, as the grains of the sands
of the sahara,
those twins had to be up to
more than bickering in the womb

like his dad he called his wife his
sister (though she was only a first
cousin) carrying the flame
of tradition, legacy of divine
right that informs evangelical
republicans today

16.37

"what is the guile of the man
without guile…?" the same

as the lie the liar doesn't tell?
same as the one
who is nothing but guile...

16.38

so the seed that spilled in sarah
rooted into the city of god,
while that which was sewn
in hagar "the bond woman"
did the opposite, as when jacob
lay his head upon the stone
and made a chrism
of christ's jism

16.39

that angel he wrestled with,
"evidently a type of christ,"
who let him win & be called
israel, who sendeth missiles
unto gaza to defend the name,
language of tyrants
and suicide attacks
and us beyond caring

16.40

and then israel sojourned into
egypt with 75 guys who hadn't
been born yet, so says the in-
fallible text being transcribed
by the fallible human, and still
siring heirs at 110 (they don't
make phalli like they used to)
went on to accomplish even
more mathematical conundra
in centuries to come

16.41

what is happening to me
vision and hearing fade
I see through frosted glass
and hear through a pillow

sequestered in my senses
as in a monk's cell
as in a prison cell–
who keeps the key?

16.42

for c.w.

a yellow schoolbus, rusting
at the edges, rattling
through the park in its dull routine,
takes your radiant and well-
loved daughterson to god

mourners criss-cross the city,
fill the synagogue, five hundred
souls murmur in the pews

those of us who have been baptized
are confused by the protocols,
but no one can resist the narrative
of this remarkable, brief, poetry-
filled life, and we weep
to the cantor's singing

the ritual without casuistry
is foreign to me, reminds me
of the smallness of this endeavor

a letter to the editor, next
day, complaining of their pronoun,
reminds me of its necessity

16.43

with abraham history reaches
puberty, the infant acquiring speech
so that it remember itself and
begin leaving its breadcrumb
trail of symbols:
the heifer, the she-goat, the ram, and
turtle-doves and pigeons that
flutter away at our
clumsy approach

next, as always, the city,
symbol of symbols,
in its sojourn, sewers
and steeples and spinning
minarets, with its tropes and its
troops, i.e.d.'s and terraces under stars,
sacred cattle and honking cars,
unimaginable grief and gutter glory,
city of gods, city of dogs, city that is
"the yoke of the law"

17.00

three shopping carts–
one from rouses, one from whole
foods, one from walgreens–
by the bench in the triangle park
on ursuline street

in the first:
a roll of black plastic sheeting,
a ruined weedeater,
a zip lock bag containing pliers and screwdriver,
a two foot length of 2x4,
a broken lamp

in the second:
a half-flat basketball,

a single shoe (converse knock-off size 6 ±),
a red toy lawnmower,
a minnie mouse backpack
stuffed full

in the third:
a mildewed pillow,
a garbage bag of moldy quilts,
a hand mirror (cracked),
a small coil of yellow romex,
a spiral notebook (pages fused)

17.01

had augustine listed every
miracle, every ominous foreshadowing,
every subtle sign of christ's coming, he
says, apologizing for his brevity,
he would still be writing today

17.02

6/16/23

now when the seed of abraham
started dispersing around *mare
nostrum* it was like the scirocco
was behind it, it was like a
meteor shower, causing kings
to bow their heads, while god
"used his temporal punishments
for training his few faithful,"
the elect having to tighten
up the rack and bear down
on the finger screws just to set
a good example,
inspiring the priests at george-
town I guess to rip those
babies from their wailing mothers'
arms and sell off the 'punic'

slaves to save from debtors
the alma mater of bill clinton,
antonin scalia and george tenet, so when sheik
abdullah bin hamad bin khalifa al thani,
deputy emir of the state of qatar,
walked in 2010, we had rather
come full circle

17.03

hagar, that "bond maid who gendereth
to bondage" also generates gender
and peels the literal
from the allegory

there is a third side, too, the
bishop claims, that goes beyond
figuration, that transcends gender
and transfigures speaking

of heaven and earth and
all such concrete matters
he assures us he's talking
about the actual things
not the words that represent them

17.04

augustine is quite en-
amored of hannah, who,
he states with prolix abandon,
can prophesy with
the best of 'em,
even if she is a girl

17.05

simply eating
bread gets complicated
with christ at the table,
and minor prophets take

turns with allegories
of food and drink,
to wine, dine
and sign
the night away

17.06

this morning she's
back at her corner
in a muscle shirt &
shorts, knobby knees
and the mangled nub,
smiling, happy

*good morning and god
bless* she says, wadding
my five-spot in her single palm,
behind the bic lighter
*what's your name? thank
you bill, I'm sistanallie... no
not allie, sister natalie...
I'll pray for you, bill, I've
got two kids,
two kids
and I'm still a virgin,
that's my story,
I'll pray for you,
bill*

& the light
changes

17.07

what is
a city?

a city is
the cloud the scirocco

brings across the sea
from hippo to rome

it is
moses' flailing,
odysseus' quest,
every myth
of being lost

it is
inscription, provenance
of identity,
text that proves
lineage, a bloodline

a nomad tribe

or that which
dreams,
psyche and structure,
fortress against invaders
or gulag for
the inner enemy

17.08

a few moments behind
the opthalmologist's laser
and the world beams in
again

in an instant
my distance
snaps back to 20-25

street signs and
office signs gleam
under the bright blue
of heaven

I had forgotten just how
crisp letters could be

17.09

these prolix passages of exegesis
bore me with their too-obvious
effort to make the texts mean
what your boss
wants them to mean

someone
or something
is fighting for its life–
against whom?

are these long quotations
followed by simple para-
phrase there to pad pages?
for the quotes can
be assigned to minions,
saving time and cramps?
can the battle be
won with sheer volume, by the literal
weight of the words?

your deadline is
your death line,
that you may be
transcribed
promptly into heaven
with that last 'amen'

17.10

"...all the kings are
called his christs..."
i.e. twice translated
once as subject,
once as object

"...consecrated with
that mystical chrism..."
the kingly
seed inside
the physical womb

"jerusalem the
bond woman"
and sarah the
free noble
whispering from
their separate beds
'...come inside me...'

17.11

this image seems
to emanate
from my groin
rather than my head,
surge of imagery
replacing the blood-
surge of youth

17.12

"...the temple of god
made of men
not of stones..."

indeed as a boy,
falling asleep during
the sermon, I could see
their faces in the walls

17.13

"...such great security is never given to any
people, that it should not dread invasions..."

rome's promise
and alaric's is
the lesson we draw
of solomon's
wise & peaceful &
imaginary reign,
lest anyone suspect
a bright spot or two
might shine, however
momentary, anywhere
along "this miserable
pilgrimage"

17.14

lord I thank you for making
a footstool of mine enemy,
sings david in the plaintive psalms,
improvising on his lute

now you smash the heads of their
children on the rocks of thy foundation,
on the stones of thy streets, till their bright
blood runs in the fossa?

david, augustine maintains, must surely
have written all the psalms,
even if he only signed
a few

17.15

the reasons why
I don't talk about all those
things I don't talk about
are legion, far
too numerous for me to list here so
that while I broach the topic
I leave you to talk about it to

yourself & move on to the next
subject I desire
to avoid

17.16

lying awake at three a.m., mind
as full of worries as
the 45th psalm with tropes...

"tropical...", a
storm of images,
torrential, surreal...

and the pirouettes he must
perform to read christ
into every phantasm...

verbal, I mean, verbal pirouettes,
if I may use a figure of speech
to obscure the quill that writes it

17.17

lifting off today to cdg, paris,
the sorbonne, either that or
days of airport hell

augustine hated sea travel
as I hate to fly, but the boss
was always calling him across
that sea full of shades,
even in his 70s, like

me, now, heeding the
call, boarding the
hated thing

17.18

augustine does
battle with the jews
upon the field of figuration

his wordplay is swordplay:
invasion, conquest, conversion
of jewish history
to christian prophecy,
interpretation by
interpenetration,
as the missionaries will do
all over africa in
centuries to come

17.19

"these words transferred
from the body signify
mental faults," he says, "...under
the prophetic form of wishing..."

prophetia,
the wish that speaks, as
opposed to that which is
wished but never spoken

"let these things which have
been said about the psalms... suffice,
that we may keep within some bound"

17.20

and david the prophet
sired that singer of
psalms who couldn't
help but inherit
the prophetic gift
but still managed to piss
away a goodly chunk

of god's blessing even while
building up carnal capital
in the song of songs,
an irresistible pleasure—
"but this pleasure is wrapped up in allegorical
veils, that the bridegroom may be more ardently
desired, and more joyfully unveiled…"

17.21

"the accomplished will of god the
avenger" sends billions to death over
one mouthful of jealous fruit but
has a hard time getting internal
affairs to check out police video when
the next black teenager takes a
bullet in the chest, like here
in france, where they killed nahel,
le marocain, in nanterre, yesterday

in paris we stumbled
onto *rue de saint augustin*,
and in rouen, *rue des augustins*, just
down the hill from jeanne d'arc's
cathedral—consecrated in 1063,
the plaque says—with its acid-
eaten gargoyles and saints,
hundreds, thousands of them patiently
waiting under the protective scaffolding
for repair and redistribution into the
moral genome

meanwhile from normandy we hear
the good news (gospel, god spiel, *bona
adnuntiatio, euangelion,* εὐαγγέλιον)
that the u.s. court has announced
its own augustinian re-pairing of
might with right

for proto-oreo
augustine & clarence thomas,
brother lackey-boys
on separate but equal
yachts, conceal their lineage as if
they'd both had the berber
beaten out of them

17.22

"seven thousand men were there
who had not bowed the knee to baal"
and seventy million who voted
against the evangelicals, but times
change and ginni thomas's
fam was surprised she was 'going with a
black man' but 'he was so nice it
made up for his being black' and
when antonin scalia explained
the power (i.e. political expedience)
of the sacrament of confession she con-
verted to the catholic and fessed
up to her admittedly child-
like admiration for the b.b.c.,
so exotic, that accent, so different
from what she grew up with

17.23

"kings arose who grievously offended
god by their impieties, and... were smitten
with moderate scourges..."
biden, for example, couldn't get student loan for-
giveness past clarence's court and besides
caught all sorts of flack over his pistol-
wielding but handsome-as-all-get-out son,
a moderate scourge if ever I heard one,
then in that other court (of public opinion)
ran neck and neck with an illiterate ogre
and eked out victory by such a slim

margin it was almost more embarrassing
than losing, all of which just has to be
punishment for some sin,
in this life or another

17.24

allegory of the allegory of the cave

now manwoman sat by its fire in its cave with its
daughterson beside it while sabre-toothed
tigers and neo-nazis with a.r.15s grumbled &
growled and barked orders outside

to distract its trembling bloodline from
the certain death at their door,
manwoman pointed at their shadows
flickering on the cave wall and told the
kid that these were the animals, that's how
insubstantial those things making the noises were,
like mere shadows, and that
manwoman and its offspring had
dominion over all the shadows,
all the animals and all the nazis
and every molecule of CO_2 in the atmosphere
and they had as well the power to name
the beasts and no beast could stand against being
named, and then it put out its hands and made
shadowhorses and shadowmen conquer
continents and cities, then changed the
story to a nursery rhyme and actually
got the kid to laugh a little
before it fell asleep, and manwoman stoked
the fire and squatted beside and kept
watch while the child slept
all the long dark night

18.01

we flee the city for
the beach in brittany, where they say
merlin turned a roman legion
into stone (though the carnac
alignments predate rome
by some millennia) and we walk,
as we all walk, among
petrified soldiers

meanwhile, putin readmits prigozhin lest
he become a russian alaric, and biden author-
izes a shipment of cluster bombs
to extract a bit more flesh
from the rejuvenated alliance, and we watch
not one but two movies in a row
that end with a guy pouring gasoline over himself
and lighting a match to hold the cop at bay

thus the city "runs its course,
not in light, but in shadow"

18.02

ninus the assyrian killed his
mother for "incestuously lying
with him," and just happened to accede
to this throne by the same gesture, while
god watched from
the shadows, augustine relates,
shaking his head at woman's
frailty

18.03

phantasms, called history, flick-
er across the page, god's
miniseries

18.04

tales of heroic men (this time
it's joseph) resisting the advances
of lustful women abound
in the city of god (which is
our topic here, he always reiterates)

not so the city I grew up in, where the guys
went around with their tongues hanging out
and told *großen lügen* about all the
pussy they were getting, tales as
short on fact as they were long on
imagery

18.05

the egyptians, augustine informs us, made
their cows horny by showing them
pictures of an alluringly spotted bull,
"just as jacob so managed with the spotted
rods that the sheep and goats were
born spotted"

not miracles, as in scripture, but historic
fact, reported by varro, no less

for augustine, you see,
there are no miracles

18.06

& if you think we
understand more
of god, history
or cities than
he did, then
you've not noticed
what you're
standing in

18.07

a relentless genealogy of kings
transformed into gods
by royal decree,
colorful context...

18.08

we survive the return
across tempestuous seas
from europe to america, crossing the
atlantic quicker than augustine crossed
mare nostrum, negotiate that hell
on earth that is the atlanta
airport, breathing prayers of
gratitude when we finally touch down
in new orleans

I remember the house as dingy,
but it appears bright and clean
when we get home, like
baudelaire's double room

the dog, whom we have missed
like a son, seems almost disappointed
to leave my son's house, with their
dog and the baby—he is healthier,
calmer, happier, than when we left him,
but his vacation from our doting
attention is over and I nap with
my arm over him

nanc forgets where she put
her glasses
just a minute ago:
'get used to it,'
she says

18.09

according to varro,
the women of athens
had the vote until
they voted against neptune
who washed away every
right and every name, even
for the "liberal" greeks, thus we have
the pagans to blame for
clarence thomas,
giorgia meloni (*femminile*
'brother of italy'), and
becki falwell, among
others, still waiting
for christ's repeal

18.10

so athena/minerva didn't get
off as cheap as it seemed
for naming rights on
the greek capital, a trend
that continues, as god
knows how much capital
caesar's put up to paint
its name on the superdome

18.11

dueling french gofundme's
raise 400k for nahel, 1.4m for
the cop who killed him

at liberty to choose
who's equal to whom, we
pick members
of our own fraternity

18.12

"in the more secret history there are said
to have been several who were called
father liber and hercules..."
and christ and augustine,
that "history" might add

if one could indeed *see* or *know*
the many motives and hands laid on
a text in its sojourn, magically, not
through the text itself, this is
the real secret,
the secret real

why "father liber"
sought the vine
in the first place

18.13

"perseus and andromeda were
raised into heaven... so that
they were not ashamed or afraid to mark out
their images by constellations"

shucking that shame they felt looking
in the mirror, & in mirror
of the sky working through
the vertigo

manwoman's vocation:
weaver, scribe, illuminator
to the stars, god's unnameable un-
known & unknowing editor

18.14

orpheus the orphan
charmed the beasts but
not so augustine, who thought him

one of those gods
"of the city of the ungodly"

widely criticized (by plato and
other phantoms) for not having
the balls to die in chasing eurydice
but slipping into hades on the sly &
still breathing

the poet charmed the pants
off of persephone till she granted him
his desire, with only this condition:
that he not look back, &

the rest is history, or as close
to his story as we will
ever be, for to know
your desire is already
to lose it

18.15

what I, like
magritte, see
in the mirror:
the back of my head

what is happening inside?
language
running its course
like a city

religion wakes
within a shell of abstraction,
far from that yellow caterpillar
tearing up the streetcorner

18.16

"they prove, not by fabulous and
poetic falsehood, but by historic attestation,
that his companions were turned into birds"

crows moving
from the cornfields
to the city make
promises future
birds can't keep

18.17

metamorphoses, lycan-
thropic or otherwise, certainly
happen all the time, though
whether in the eye
of the beholder or the flesh
of the beheld is an argument
for another city

this quasi-scientific analysis of
quasi-mystical events allays doubts
about both science and mysticism,
but leaves only politics with
which to weave the narrative

18.18

"...landladies of inns,
imbued with these wicked arts..."
spike the cheese with border scenarios,
fondle apulieus's golden ass, & generally
try to make goods of god's
promises, so manwoman learned
to trust neither ladies nor cheese,
consulting plato on matters
of substance and appearance, circe
on metamophoses, and, on matters
of court, the birds

of the temple of diomede, who bringeth
water in their beaks to comfort
the greeks while they
torment aliens

18.19

a meticulous accounting
of transactions along the
mediterranean coastline
from rome to old hippo
will yield the real
(adjusted for inflation)
value of the handful of coins
I drop into the styrofoam cup
in the hand
of the elderly black man
sitting on his walker
at claiborne and esplanade
this morning,
as well as the prices
his ancestors and mine
paid for and to each other
for the past four
millennia, and the chump
change ($22,500,
in today's dollars) trump's
billionaire buddies
are dropping for a
seat and a plate of
crappy chicken cordon bleu
at the metairie
country club tonight,
charity to fund the
putsch they're setting
up for 2024

18.20

at tulane and broad
across from the courthouse
two budding orators
one on a mr. microphone
one on a megaphone
call and response
like an echo
middle of the work day
'I know I know
some of you are asking
asking what what
should I do with myself do
with myself but if you ask just
ask god what to do
if you ask god to see
you through see you
through then you're gonna do
gonna do what you set out set out
to do whatever you
set out to do that's what
that's what you'll do'

18.21

augustine, liberal in his
censure of false gods,
is conservative in treatment
of his own

so it is with most
who call fellow
humans & estranged
gods fools

18.22

"...rome was founded, like another babylon, and as it were the daughter of the former babylon, by which god was pleased to conquer the whole world..."

city of god, city of
ungod, both
end up rome,
manwoman
daughterson, godhead
giving head
and the species comes

18.23

"...Ἰησοῦς Χριστὸς Θεοῦ υἱὸς σωτήρ,...
'jesus christ the son of god,
the saviour'... as translated by some
one into latin in good rhythm," he says,
then by dods and then by me,
in this summer of wildfires, 2023

what the sibyl said:

I I douse the earth with my standard—
H hero we shall never be rid of
Σ sent to judge at the end of the world
O of believing and faithless alike,
Y youth and age sisted before him

X xtians decimate the planet,
P rotate idols and dig up treasures—
E earth, consumed by fire,
I intimates the portals of hell—
Σ some souls inherit freedom but
T the guilty, as usual, burn forever, while
O occult publications reveal silly

Σ secrets of the heart—
Θ there'll be wailing, gnashing of teeth,
E eclipse of the sun, stars silenced—
O over is moonlight, molten the heavens,
Y valleys rise up, mountains lie down,

Y youth recedes
I into the distance, skies & oceans merge
O on the end of all things! the broken earth
Σ swells with burning rivers

Σ sound of a trumpet's peal
Ω over these who groan in their guilt—
T torture and trembling, hell on earth—
H here where kings stand to be judged
P resplendent flames fall from heaven

18.24

'have a good day, hear?'
he (the beggar from 1.11)
yells to each car as it passes,
cardboard sign reading 'anything
helps' around his neck, looking and
feeling his eighty or thereabouts years,
and to those who drive by without
a glance he screams with rage,
'god bless you, hear?'

18.25

augustine constructs in
his history parallel
timelines for rome and
israel, from adam to him-
self, the point where, he
imagines, they converge

four years after he finishes
de civitate dei contra paganos,
in 430, the pagans (vandals) come
to hippo regius—bull helmets, daimons
dancing by firelight outside the city walls—
& augustine, at 75, dies
in the year-long siege

the vandals held the city
till 534, when east rome
took it back, then came
the arabs in 698,
bringing islam, decimating
all the old haunts

the berbers, scattered &
outlawed by both
rome & its enemies,
remembered
neither in scripture nor
history, barely endured, yet
the ogress, older
than noah, older than
adam, still walked
the streets & dreams of old
annaba when the next wave of
latin missionaries
(spanish and french)
came ashore

did she visit augustine, wayward
son, in his final hours?
did she come forward, foetid
mother, to save him from his
salvation?

18.26

as most any prophet
might have predicted,
four months after
the mardi gras cleanup,
when they loaded tarps and
furnishings into garbage trucks
with yellow tractors, and
citizens into police vans
with yellow warrants,
the tent cities are again

sprawling under the interstates
and nungesser has not
gotten his gaily painted screens
nor his portable toilets

the settlement on claiborne stretches five
blocks, with its own streets and alleys,
its own commerce and
civil society

what do we prophesy
of its fate?

18.27

in times of trans-
ition, these inter-
stices between empires,
when the old city
wanes and a new
one waxes, prophets flower
and spread,
set off with their
shopping carts
for new neighborhoods,
speaking in tongues, speaking
in a language that
never had to be learned

18.28

"we should but weaken the savour of
this prophetic oracle if we set ourselves
to expound it," yet this vision of hosea
textually convulsing on the
figural ground en-
thralls so completely
that the saint must append two
pages of what resembles nothing
so much as exposition

but no sibyl in deep
trance was ever more
enthralled by a god than augustine
by the gnosis of regular old
expository prose

18.29

"yet I think those parts sufficient
which are so plain that even enemies
must be compelled against their will
to understand them," letters so
clear, calligraphy so perfect, analogies
so compelling, rhythm so
hypnotic that even pagans
must nod in agreement

18.30

jonah, on the other
hand, prophesied without words,
for he was "taken into the whale's
belly and restored on the third day,"
brought back from the bardo,
where signs don't signify
but signal similitude

18.31

academic, priest, senator, judge, mayor,
property manager, archivist & livestock
inspector in one, aug-
ustine mastered
the ancient esoteric
art of bureaucratic
schmoozing, finally making
councilman at
civitas dei

18.32

running short on
"spiritual supplies" despite the
proliferation of prophets and
miracles... how many fucking
falls and floods do we
have to have before
finally rising into that
dopamine bliss of salvation?

18.33

jeremiah appears
to have farmed some of his
prophecy to his secretary,
but this by no means should
diminish its authority, for the servant
takes the dictation of the master
just as the master has taken it
from god, and if servant or master
inserts a word or two of their (sup-
posed) own, there is no reason to assume
that word is not every bit as divinely
inspired as the rest

18.34

in the alley
behind the millshop,
back behind the garbage
cans, someone screaming, & we
find this guy incoherent, like
a sibyl in trance, sounds
emanating from his throat that
sound neither of any throat nor
of any known speech, & he sways and
squats and
leaps up, crazed,
does it again

doug calls 911:
is he violent? hard to say, though
we don't want to get any closer—
responsive? again, hard to say, though
we can't get his attention—
description? white male, five foot eight,
black hair and beard, shirtless,
tattoos on chest and arms,
khaki shorts and
boots, that's all he's
wearing, hear that do you
hear him you should be able
to hear him now he's
screaming?

I don't want
to deal with cops, no
matter what kind of prophet
we have here, &
head on
back to work

18.35

by the time we get
to haggai, zechariah, and
malachi I've had
enough of prophets and your
cataloging of every instance
where with benefit of hindsight
we might interpret the vague
symbols as standing for jesus...

for these parables could as
well predict hitler or
trump as
christ

18.36

what courses through my
mind as I lie awake this night?
bits of song, musical refrains that
repeat endlessly, movie scenes, whether I
want them to or not, 'images' remembered or
conjectured, screens of emails or poems
materializing, euphoric imaginings of
playing guitar or building the screen porch,
I 'write' songs and poems from
the safety of the bed (sometimes
remembering sometimes not),
& sometimes I get up and truly
write them, and sometimes
merely imagine I do

and what coursed through augustine's
head, two thousand years ago?
script and scripture, turns of phrase,
feel of the quill in his hand and sinuous
track of the letters, does he sometimes
get up and light the lamp to capture
a particular rhetorical flourish before
it drifts away? does he question, as I,
this very process, feel the thoughts
squirming in his head like demons
in the air? does he 'see' himself lying
in the bed and feel death approaching
and think he must, absolutely must,
finish this work, this construction,
citadel of language, before his time arrives?

though there is nothing
to fear in death, of course

18.37

3 august, 2023
trump's 3rd arraignment

each charge sparks
a surge in the polls
as fake news of
fake news arrives
via x, consoling evangelical
xtians everywhere that filthy
rich americans prefer them believing
what they want to believe,
for what they lack believing
they gain pretending

18.38

"... the ark he made, in which
he escaped with his family,
was itself a prophecy of our time..."
just as the child's
toy boat prefigured
the ark, and the floating
leaf that

but let's not venture
too far back
into this etymology,
for prophecy is not
sign but iteration

jeremiah predicts, first
of all, that others will
predict

it will be augustine
who finally learns
to make a sign
sing

18.39

heber bests isis
in the semiotic arm-
wrestle by weight
of the hebrew letters,
appointing *inductores*
to "introduce them
into the hearts of learners"

the saint maintains that hebrew
letters existed before the words
that contain them, but
cautions against reliance
on omens that are too old,
some might have expiry
dates, some might be
"mere astronomy"

18.40

as to the claim that egypt
was superior in any way
(astronomically, philosophically,
militarily or histrionically)
to "our" forebears, we have it by
divine decree that our
diviners, astrologists, fore-
casters and jailers are
number one in every category

varro even maintains that, could we
execute a time warp and have
a futbol match between us now,
we would win handily, and go on
to heaven besides, and they'd
still be stuck in pyramids, but these
"things in secular books... whether true
or false, yield nothing of moment
to our living rightly and happily"

18.41

yet caution, "lest on account of their multitude
what ought to be religiously esteemed
should grow cheap"—inflation in the
spiritual sphere affects material markets,
thus we reveal the divine
knowledge prophet by prophet,
with control, releasing a letter
at a time, to avoid market
saturation

"...certain philosophers, amid
their false opinions, were able
to see that god has made
this world, and himself
most providently governs it,
or of the nobility of the virtues,
of the love of country,
of fidelity in friendship,
of good works and everything
pertaining to virtuous manners..."

christ, *die große lüge*,
christ *die größte lüge*

18.42

augustine relates it was ptolemy philadelphus,
the egyptian, who requested
the translation of the scriptures,
so the twelve tribes each
sent him 6 translators—
the famous, if approximate, septuagint—
and philadelphus, just as a test,
had them each work in isolation

72 little scribing cells, silent but for
the scratching of the quills and
the clinking of the inkwells,

each produced its testament, and
"they differed from each other in no word"

18.43

yet even in this field of perfect
concordance there were moments
in which the two might "... say the same thing
differently, so that, although the words
were not the same, yet the same meaning
should shine forth"

later, they inserted "certain marks
in the form of stars
which they call asterisks"
to announce sections of the original
the 72 translators, as one, decided
to leave out, and also indicated by
"horizontal spit-shaped marks like
those by which we denote ounces" what
the 72 translators, in unison, elected
to append

18.44

and of that instance
in which the one says three
and the other forty, the septuagint
(plus two) no doubt have opted
to keep the inattentive reader
on its toes, making up its own
mind whether the symbol refers to
resurrection or ascension

"and this may admonish the
reader not to despise the authority
of either, but to raise himself above
the history, and search for those things
which the history itself was
written to set forth"

18.45

when israel lost its prophets
it lost its profits too, with all manner
of romans and ptolemys rifling
its stores, until the "expectation
of the nations," with great
irony, was symbolized
by a virgin expecting

and what do nations ironically
expect today? is it qanon
or *the matrix* or chatgpt that
casts our bones, that drinks
our blood for soothsay?

18.46

and so came
such an one,
sin semilla,
who made the sibyl's
prophecies come
true and confused
the jews so thoroughly
they scattered
and left the battlefield,
and "we" started to laud
their lord for he had
had the foresight,
with romans and
proud boys
closing in,
to abandon them

18.47

job proves by example
you don't have to be jewish
to be eligible for the sacred
torture in the heavenly city,

and, lest anyone think
xtians forged their
foreshadowings or
their foreskins,
here is the signature
on the scripture

18.48

this new church of
"living stones" is ever
more defensible than
the old one, it quells
rome's fury by joining up,
doing as it does,
for just as a body
enjoys to lie in luxury,
so doth a church

18.49

rome's latin solved
the babel/babble problem and let
those early parables sojourn
tongue to tongue in language not
greek to its listeners and certainly
not hebrew so they called it cath-
olic which means
everyone
worth bothering with

18.50

then came the preachers,
singly and in teams, and
"the blood of the martyrs...
poured forth..."

they set up tents
in the desert and held
revivals, saving the slaves

from pagan owners
so they could build
nicer churches
for their new ones, in
rome & paris &
new orleans

18.51

"the city of confusion"
appears on the horizon
approaching full of heretics,
who, apparently, writhe full
of sins too subtle to catalog yet
nonetheless egregious, "con-
tumaciously" roadblocking
civitas dei in its travels

but this is profitable for
us,
keeps us agile and witty,
our argument muscles toned, and
if it cause us a bit of grief,
a sleepless night
or two, well
cain did slay abel

18.52

desantis himself descends
to the heresy: trump lost!
how will it play with
the congregation?

checkbooks at the ready,
they await the passing of the plate

what a feather in the cap
of the super rich, to have this

genius in their pocket
but does he have a prayer?

no one wants
to back a loser

the sermon riffs on moses
parting the waters &
watching them close again
over the heads of the enemy

18.53

"some say four hundred, some
five hundred, others a thousand
years, may be completed
from the ascension...
to his final coming"

and some said 365,
a year of years (on
the roman calendar) till
the antichrist, at least
that was the thinking two
thousand years ago,
so you can't blame me if the
city of confusion settles over me
too like a cloud, homespun
teleology

18.54

in the sullen heat of
an august evening, I
walk the dog by the gaping
maw and broken windows
of an abandoned house,
now given over to crack

odors of mildew

and piss and burnt
wood emanate from the
openings, demonic
breath from
city's inner being

in the rubble of the unfenced yard
a guy is holding a mangy
german shepherd by the scruff—
I mumble hello awkwardly—
'that white dude
talked to us' he says
to the dog

I move on quickly,
fearing for my little terrier
against his cerberus,
for here in new orleans
"the two cities…
are mingled together"

19.00

mid-summer doldrums
crepe myrtles drop
their purple petals
which lie in heaps
in the gutter or
clutter the hoods
and windshields of
the cars

the dog must drink
or spread-eagle on
the cooler grass
in the shade

he drinks from my hand
starts drinking
before I even pour

half of it runs
through my fingers
darkening
the cracks in the sidewalk

no reason to be here
or elsewhere, I live
in language, virtual
and real, a long-dead half-
imaginary saint
as close to me as the
friend next door

19.01

8/7/23

"...the reasonings by which men
have attempted to make for themselves
a happiness in this unhappy life..."

288 possible solutions, varro
reckons, 288 sects ("not that
have actually existed... but
which are possible") or ways of vainly
seeking "a happiness"
but does not count the passion for
the catalog as one, nor augustine's
logophilia, nor (I venture to guess)
sister natalie's (17.04) chastity, nor just
getting up and doing your thing every
day with no more thought of *beatus*
than of a bear cub loose on on a plane
(which happened in dubai this morning)

19.02

this bear,
"primary object of nature"
landing on an iraqi air flight

from baghdad, spectacle
and plaything for filthy
rich oil men—whether the cute
little fur ball distracts the sheiks
from the human misery it so cutely
represents long enough to qualify
as a "supreme good" or if it remains
just an everyday diversion neither
varro nor augustine
venture to speculate

19.03

virtue virtually
leaves its competition for supreme
good in the dust, showing everyone
from aristotle to zizek
a solution so self-apparent no proof
need be offered

does the soul use
virtue like the man his horse?
or contain it like the cup
its water?

these points are for
angels to argue, and they don't care
if you dress like a cynic
(that is, gutter punk) or not

19.04

'the lord knoweth the thoughts
of the wise,' sayeth paul, mis-
quoting the psalm, 'that they
are vain'

not even cicero can wrap his
rhetoric around "the miseries
of this life," which is a miniseries

of sickness amputation deafness
blindness delirium and in-
sanity something like
this poem

and what does the city of god
have to say about the matter?
pretty much what any city
says about anything:
be patient
be prudent
be polite

19.05

and society of fellows?
he continues in
kierkegaardian fervor,
companionship of
citizens and philosophers
wives concubines and chattels
no matter how much comfort
they give the contemplative
aristocrat, invariably spin
down into "enmity as bitter
as the amity was sweet"

next thing you know
ukraine's getting leveled
and civil war in niger

19.06

we pity the poor judges "compelled
to put innocent witnesses to the
torture to ascertain the truth" &
must carry such sin in their
wretched conscience and pass
it on to descendents at guantánamo

19.07

"...the imperial city has endeavoured
to impose on subject nations not only
her yoke but her language"
which is the more substantial
for you can buy or hack yourself
out of chattel but the language
owns you and yours
forever

19.08

"we enjoy some gratification
when our good friends die"
for if truth be told
they weren't really that
good to start with
but I listened to you
I inherited your speech

19.09

and then if you grow tired of
all this human frailty and pick a
god or two for companion
you quickly discover them to be
every bit as gossipy &
malicious as you are

like if they made you they
made you just like them
or if you made them you
made them just like you

either way

19.10

"virtue makes a good use
even of the evils a man suffers"

whereas for woman man makes
evil use of the virtue she represents

but as to the matter of woman
getting a little *beatus* herself
augustine feels no need
to comment

19.11

for the wicked to suffer their
proper punishment (endless)
they have to live forever & this proves
the immortality of even their souls
thus the saints lying around up there
in "eternal peace" get a peep
show that makes them feel special

19.12

"pride in its perversity apes
god" yet what ape doesn't
long for the pleasures of the perverse
for the lamb to beat up on the lion
or the kite to be
eaten by a corpse, the
contra naturam
of the natural order

19.13

"the peace of the celestial city
is the perfectly ordered and
harmonious enjoyment
of god, and of one another in god"

as the patrician enjoys his plebes
and the plebe looks up
at the patrician,
enjoying one another

19.14

for the celestial city is
"the well-ordered concord of those...
who rule and those who obey"
rome without police
law without violation
but there is no law without
violation (it's a secret)
no rome without
police (also secret)

19.15

"it is with justice, we believe, that
the condition of slavery is the result of sin"

all servitude is penal
all slaves guilty &
the old testament a manual
for the construction of roman
roads and bridges
as well as mississippi
cotton plantations

19.16

paterfamilias becomes *praetor civitas,*
forced march to *praetoria*
to protect the natural order

19.17

celestial city surrounds
the earthly as new orleans the
tent town on claiborne
or paris nanterre
and deploys the *polis*
in the event of insurrection
unsightly accumulation and/
or rodentia

19.18

one thing about
the city of god
what it knows
it knows
there is no
doubting scripture
it has no history
no provenance
no relation to
anything but itself
absolute certainty
unrelenting unwavering
faith

19.19

so long as it's "nothing
indecent or self-indulgent"
you are free to dress
as you please in the holy
city, that's right you can
slouch like an old hippy, ratty
t-shirt and blue jeans, or
get dolled up in sunday-
go-to-meetin' or just put on your
favorite guayabera and some
comfortable linen pants
to contemplate in style

19.20

"now blessed, though not in reality
so much as in hope" like
desantis and pence and for that
matter the corporate bodies
that fund their "hope"

19.21

cicero wields
the "weal of the people"
in his faked republic
but this text leaves no
scar upon the civil
body (which is made
of people as people
are made of cells)

19.22

god may be all powerful and quite
sufficient unto himself but
that doesn't mean he can't appreciate
the yummy smell from your grill
when you fire up the burgers and
thighs of a sunday afternoon

that smoke wafting up toward
heaven would make any self-
respecting god's mouth water, unlike,
say, the wildfires scorching the
earth at lahaina this week,
where the meat you smell
is the citizens and the smoke
seems to follow no matter
where you stand

19.23

"...we ourselves, who are his own city,
are his most noble and worthy sacrifice,
and it is this mystery we celebrate in our sacrifices..."

just as jonah (18.30) signified christ mimetically
the lamb we throw on the fire signifies our-
selves metonymically, as the lamb lies down
in the city of the lion

19.24

but the curl of live flesh on the fire
and concomitant yummy smells
if offered up in profligacy
turn the republic republican
and next thing you know
alaric's chowing down
augustine wags his finger
trump tightens his tie

19.25

god gets jealous if people invite
apollo and company to the barbecue
so jealous that he changes
the definition of people (for god
is master of language too) to include
only republicans and launches "sanguinary
seditions" saying the steaks are too rare
our host hasn't done due
diligence, & the grand jury
in georgia hands down the indictment
so we're about to see which god
man or hero gets
sacrificed now

19.26

here in this our south
"—the temporal peace which the
good and the wicked together enjoy"
settles over us and the states turn
red not from republicans but
the weather—you could sacrifice
your lamb right on the sidewalk
today in baton rouge and
that tent city of ungodly poor people
under the interstate writhes and
shrinks under god's spatula

19.27

"witness the prayer of the whole
city of god in its pilgrim state,
for it cries to god by the
mouth of all its members"

19.28

do you think about her
now and then—
the concubine who
in all your scribbling you
never name—do you
remember fucking, sworn off
pleasure, & pleasure even
more so for bring foresworn,
sacred virginity's
shameful end?
did your mother
bring her to you,
thoughtful gift, or left-
over pagan ritual?
did you whisper
to adeodatus
growing in her belly?
were you able to resist
her body in that moment
of its fullness?
what bitter regret,
what ancient grief & what
vengeful longing calls up
these images of
hell on earth?

20.01

we speak not
of the last day but
of the very last…
a day without hours

no sun rises nor sets
nor moon nor stars
nor planets look down
upon it but christ
with his standard
proud white boy face &
hippy hair rises yet again
to "judge the quick
and the dead" and all us
guilty quick shall writhe in
agony like some now-
forgotten berber tribe
forced into a cave for
suffocation, or like the last
wretched citizens
of a conquered city being
loaded onto cattle cars,
whips and razor wire rend
the flesh of the faithful
torture and wailing like
in a moroccan
prison rain down
from the god of
due diligence

20.02

good falls to evil &
evil to good which "seems
unjust" but that's just
because we can't see
the big picture
and when christ
comes back to give
everyone their just
deserts then we'll see
just how lucky he was
to be crucified and just
how close to hell it would be
to live at mar-a-lago

20.03

the fact that solomon
"the wisest man"
coined "all is vanity"
or even that he is assumed to
proves it to be so
for '...how dieth the wise
man? as the fool...'

20.04

"I shall first, then, state the case,
and then call the witnesses"
he says in
opening argument
setting precedent
for perry mason and giuliani
proving the validity
of last judgment
by making it

20.05

for the present intermingles
what the future shall
sequester:
god is here &
your desire
just happens
to coincide
to your prophecy

20.06

"let those who are dead in soul
bury them that are dead in body"
might have already come
true if we can judge by the
crowd of deadheads cheering
(the late) jerry garcia on

youtube, quickly buried under
a dumptruck load of ads,
which we contemplate
in memory of youth:
'how did we miss this?'

20.07

now that the millenium which john
promised until judgment day
has twice passed, we again
contemplate our teleology with
"ridiculous fancies" and glossolalia
rakes in cash via
the tv portal (evangelista
sweating through her second
skin of makeup makes a
language of five syllables that
need no translation
even to foreigners) &
secures funding for lawsuits
against the epa, so
we won't have to wait
another thousand for that
"second resurrection"

20.08

and never think that one day
the church will pass away
no matter how fervently the
devil be loosed upon us
no matter how devilish
the details nor how pin-
point accurate the aim
of his swat team here comes
the slaughter &
the laughter

20.09

back to my 'roots' in
arkansas where christ and
trump and gun rights
rule the yard signs
I see 'joe and da hoe gotta
go' on a t-shirt at the bar and drunk
I tell the guy that's the most obscenely
racist slogan I have seen in a
state full of obscenely racist slogans
and he says thank you

dave says I
should retire back there
that it's peaceful
but I guess I'll
ride out this particular
judgment day here in
new orleans
where the saints, despite
obvious gaps in the
o-line, still reign

20.10

the resurrection
will not be televised—
why I doubt
there'll even be
a podcast

20.11

when gog the carpenter and
magog the roofer come
to your town they enclose
without limit
no matter your
insurance
they are everywhere

at once shingling
like a language
not a city not a nation but
a language an end
to every delay
to every hem and haw

20.12

death of siegfried

an ostensible prigozhin
falls from the sky to feel
the "firmness of the firmament"
putin rules, really? that fear-
less warrior so easily tricked?
do we need dragon's blood
to see through putin's lie?
whether or not, what do
we imagine happens now
to the wagner dwarves
seeded across the earth
(russia belarus serbia syria
sudan mozambique central african republic
mali niger libya sudan madagascar haiti) still
listening for *siegfried*'s horn call
&, with no one around to sign
paychecks on friday, in need of
gainful employment?

20.13

doing the math, it appears
that the reign of the saints
and of the antichrist shall
overlap by a period of precisely
42 months during which
god is a bit vague as to
exactly what will happen but
looking back (for it came

to pass a thousand years
ago) looks suspiciously like
any other 42 months

20.14

"and this divine power
is called a book"
i.e. a magical history in which
all is laid out for god
to surveil in a glance
kicking the sinful into the fire
and stowing the good ones
in the heavenly library

that is to say, one scribbles
or one's scribes scribble
for the sole purpose
of making those scribbles
disappear

20.15

while augustine relates some
of the finer points of the eternal
suffering to come, our
lame duck governor edwards
floats a bill to give some
modest sinners a get out of
hell free card, but the pop-
ulace rises up in anonymous
polling to smite the measure
down: they may not be able
to witness live video of black
guys getting their heads chewed
off in the ninth circle of angola,
but just knowing
it's all happening behind
the razor wire lets them breathe
a sigh of relief

20.16

writing is a false god, as
"...the surging and restlessness
of human life..." wrestles
with the metaphor of the
mother, crown jewel of
sentiments, and finds itself
"symbolized by the sea"

20.17

our saint finds it
"excessively barefaced"
(inpudentiae nimiae)
to read the apocalypse
literally, like our own
impudent oil execs buying
up wind leases just
so they can lie fallow
while it rains fire,
'climate talks' in nice hotels
yield barefaced good wishes,
wheat crops cook in the ground &
trump's barefaced mugshot
hits every front page, and
the worst is yet to come

20.18

peter weighs in
with a view of the end
in which the atmosphere
turns to "moisture" and the entire
sensory frame melts
like a dali landscape or an acid
trip from your youth

in the next pane the usual
mortals in agony cry
out of the usual conflagration

but this is of no concern
to the saints for they
remember that three men
stood in the furnace
and were not consumed

20.19

what paul said to the thess-
alonians is tricky to decode but
tradition says the church is the
antichrist and all the people inside
mini-antichrists playing hide
& seek in the pews and at night
among the headstones
in the cemetery out back, no doubt
there'll be a trumpet blast
hunter's horn lowing across
the valley at dawn a rifle flash
and I had the warm blood
of a hart on my hands

20.20

she speaks of nausea and
dizziness after supper while
I feel fine, we google the
symptoms: heart attack
it says

I downplay, google searches
favor the sensational, I scoff
though my heart beats
faster please god don't
let her go first

20.21

"...but because there shall thence flow,
even upon earthly bodies, the peace
of incorruption and immortality, therefore

he says that he shall flow down as this
river, that he may as it were pour himself
from things above to things beneath..."

20.22

and the good even as they lounge
in their "happy abodes" shall
have also the pleasure of wit-
nessing the torments of their wicked
counterparts, all without leaving
the comfort of the heavenly couches,
& neither on netflix nor youtube but
by telepathic knowledge, by
simply knowing, in mind's
eye shall the blesséd view
"the worm that dieth not,
and the fire that is not quenched,"
and they shall hear the cries of the
sinners in their eternal torment
without having to actually "go"
to that sad place

20.23

like the proverbial mouse that casts
the shadow of a dragon,
this temporal existence projects
itself as an eternal morality
to scare predators away

20.24

certain "men ... shall be
caught up to meet christ
in the air," on the spiritual
roller coaster ride,
(raise your hands
at the top of the climb
for the most exquisite vertigo,)
but in the end this isn't

any dumber than faith in
one's fellow mortals,
that fickle god
'community'

20.25

9/9/23

the local archdiocese launches
a gofundme to pay legal fees &
restitution to those few (well,
500) profligate boys & girls
hannon successors and
assigns diddled in the course
of shepherding their flocks,
so drop an extra dollar
in the plate this sunday
that the tradition may
be saved, and remember
as he said in 1.25, so
long as they didn't actually
enjoy it, the kids should be
ok in heaven's tally and join
the priests themselves
in the blessed city

20.26

9/11

allah 'akbar—
so he was
22 years ago
and 2 days too
in marrakech
for those "...banished thence
on account of their
transgression" (for neither christ
nor fellow *große lüge* allah

would muss their robes
with such messy work)
and agadir in 1960
and gaza and eastern
ukraine today,
fields of destruction
we can justly
blame on gods

20.27

"such a judgment as has never
before been," a vision augustine
shares with clarence thomas who
lies awake at night itching to sink
his pen into anything that smacks
of 'right to privacy' (though just try
to sneak a camera on one of those
yachts) for it is just those privy
moments we need to
be punished for

20.28

& regardless of all the cruelly
inequitable sentences handed
down in the course of history
by judges both human and divine
showering honor glory wealth and offspring
upon liars thieves and murderers
and poverty prison and sorrow without bound
upon the most saintly and selfless among us
the "last" judgment shall be the perfect
pairing of every mortal (living or not)
with the just punishment and/or
eternally blessed sensual massage
everything so equitable
there will be no need to ever
judge anything again

20.29

even the "carnal"
jews will get the message
when elias comes to town
like in an episode of
gunsmoke (the old thirty-minute
black & white version) they'll be
saved at the very last
second, prophecy or
childhood memories
rerun as metaphors

20.30

"the almighty sent the almighty"
into the language lending it
iterability, subject transiting
object like the murderer
threatening the mirror,
christ and the bourgeois cry out:
god god why have I forsaken you?
mortals sentenced to pronouns,
case and gender

21.00

botero (1932-2023)

form filled out, highest
expression of the
carnal, hagar's line
described by vectors, compass
point at the navel
another on the nose,
bodymind of quiet discretion,
longing to embrace to be
surrounded and absorbed

21.01

toni loses her
gig at the con-
struction company
(she trained an assistant
and then they
fired her) &
goes homeless
she and the kid
sleeping in
her car
beth drives
over to austin
to see
if she can get her
back on her feet &
out of the casino
starts a gofundme
for a room
hoping to forestall
her moving in—
jesus christ toni we laughed
and sang in our cups
that mardi gras
so sure I'll drop
a c-note
on the plate but
would give way more to see
you laugh again,
little prankster,
little cynic
like me
salvation came &
went for us

21.02

in this particular rhet-
orical flourish the

saint plays devil's
advocate so well the
devil wins

21.03

if it ever ended it wouldn't be
hell, is the argument for im-
mortality of the soul, or actually
body, since hell requires physical fuel, but

when the human
crackles like bacon
"the soul is so connected with the body
that it succumbs to great pain and withdraws"
only to be returned like a bug on a
string that it may rejoin the flesh
in suffering for eternity

& we need to make this argument
expeditiously for "our opponents"
will be knocking
very soon now

21.04-05

of hell and language—

"*this fire is kindled
when it is extinguished*"

he read that a certain
salamander lives happily in fire

the peacock steak he pushed away
and left on his desk for years
suffered no degradation

he saw a magnet held beneath a
plate move a piece of iron above

he heard that in cappadocia
the wind impregnates mares

in arcadia asbestos burns &
cannot be put out

the salt of agrigentum turns to
water in fire and into fire in water

the garamantæ fountain is freezing
cold by day, scalding at night

& the apples of sodom turn to ash
when touched by hand or tooth

all signs that
eternal suffering awaits

21.06

this writing which ex-
tinguishes the inextinguishable
and ignites the incombustible,
which creates the "iron image"
and forecasts the reign of fire,
writing "we are bound to believe"
has no physical existence,
could as well have been
"other words with the same
meaning," *contra paganos*
with the pagans at the gate
of the physical hippo regius,
city of god with its spirit
barricaded inside,
which will shortly be ending
its sojourn in africa, for
the vandal, too, is
a wanderer

21.07

the lump

panic spreads through
the family, chills running up
the collective spine

just when our minds
seem least capable—
your house or ours?
live-in nurse? (will
insurance pay?)
hospice?

you will forgo
chemo, you
don't fear dying, you
say, but do fear
dying badly

witchcraft, spirits
in the æther,
spells cast 50 and 100
and two thousand years ago again
swirl in the mist
and we are entranced

you don't want anyone
but your sons,
you have them ask me
and your sisters
to stay away

21.08

venus shifts her orbit
just this once
to prove "human bodies will
always burn and yet never die"

for natures can change
no matter how writ in stone
they may seem

a person might walk
their dog to the park every
morning at 6 a.m. for a thousand
days but wake one morning and
not

the sun may rise & set &
shine for a million years
yet today it may not

21.09

10/10/2023

and speaking of burning
forever, the "worm that dieth
not" sticks its head out
of the flames and invites us
to jump in to the action
today in gaza, where
missiles numbering
as the grains of the sahara
rain down on apartments, hospitals
schools and prisons, and prayers in
the several languages of the children
of abram lift up to heaven imploring
their various gods to make
their neighbors' present
suffering æternal

21.10

"one fire certainly
shall be the lot of both"
mystically speaking (that is,

speaking period)
the same lake of fire awaits
on either side
of the no-go zone, whether
you're from gaza or tel aviv,
it even appears sometimes
that the victor's side burns
a little hotter
than the vanquished pilgrim's,
& the bourgeois on both banks
mop their brows with the same ex-
asperated motion

21.11

augustine proves
god's law just
by analogy to the roman—
our eternal punishment follows
the precedent
of the "many years confinement
imposed on the slave who
has provoked his master,"
though god's imperium outranks
the civil slave owner, of course,
so our sentence need not be
limited to life

21.12

10/21/23

twenty truckloads of bread
water and bandaids are allowed
to breach the siege line and
enter gaza from egypt,
a huge diplomatic victory &
the right thing to do from a
humanitarian perspective though
the relief they bring

to the six million souls
be like the proverbial glass
of water in hell

eternal punishment
for the sin of a moment—
this is the standard
set by god

21.13

plato and virgil
are proponents of purgatory
but augustine reminds us
no amount of heaving
will ever expel
that famous first bite

21.14

your son looks
for you this morning & for a moment
fears you might have wandered
away in the night, your
withered body barely
perceptible under the
blanket on the bed

the oncologist has
washed his hands

your abdomen fills
with black bile,
they could drain it,
they say, but
it will only refill

augustine says of sons:
"the learning to which they are driven
by punishment is itself so much

of a punishment to them, that they
sometimes prefer the pain that drives them
to the pain to which they are driven by it"

and I wonder what memories
might prompt a guy in his
seventies
to write such a strange
sentence as that

21.15

'civilians'
heeding netanyahu's call,
flee the borderlands
'the widening war' & the
'unimaginable force'
about to be unleashed, for
"now in its misery it
makes war upon itself"
as the body as-
pires to the civil

21.16

10/23/23

you passed this morning,
our son tells me on the phone,
it would feel weird, he says,
not to, but if I want
to see you come
now as you'll be going
straight to cremation

the four of them, your
sons and daughters-in-law,
sitting around the living room,
get up one by one to hug me
as I walk in, then

I look down and see the
feet protruding from a blanket
I thought was simply
thrown over a chair, only
then do I see you, head lolled side-
ways mouth agape, beth
beside you holding your
hand under the blanket,
an involuntary 'oh shit' es-
capes me as I jump back

then ben shows me a photo
of a blastocyst

21.17

like high school jocks
having fun with a sissy,
brothers augustine and
jerome tease and taunt old
origen for his being
so "merciful" as to
suggest our punishment might be
something less than æternal:
"...he does indeed put to shame
their charity, but is himself convicted
of error that is more unsightly,
and a wresting of god's truth
that is more perverse, in proportion as
his clemency of sentiment seems to be"

21.18

it is not spirit that haunts
but your body, its
munchian last attitude
as its warmth evaporated

I watched your progress
from youth to decrepitude

and learned some things
along the way

'I am not afraid'
you said, *erste lüge*,
the innate lie
of speaking at all

not, let us pray,
"...holding out false hopes"
for "...this quasi compassion
of god to the whole race"

21.19

at the remembrance

the three 'adopted daughters' huddle
on things past
& on arrangements going forward

we all get drunk and
laugh and try on
your jewelry and hats

old men arrive from a past
that was dim on a good day

distant generations
of friends, relatives, work-
mates, strike up conversations
over your curios

everyone says
you would have liked it

21.20

augustine and company don't
capitalize catholic

even now when the church
is selling off real estate to pay
the pederasty fines (adding some
lovely inventory to
the city's stock of historic
b&bs along the way) but
with our new priest-speaker mike (johnson)
now capitalizing the capitol,
let's open with a prayer
we remember to spell shit right

21.21

off-grid at big sur
contemplating a nature neither
berber saint nor beat poet
could have imagined

five miles up the road we suddenly
get a signal and pent up
messages and news feeds
condense out of the æther

israel is calling hamas's bluff,
bombing the refugee camps
where they have sheltered—
in absence of cell towers & electricity the
hellfire rains down without warning

dinner at nepenthe with its stunning
sunset view, just down the coast from
silicon valley, where they've made
so much money from phones
they don't need to carry them
and enjoy nature *au naturel*

california wine:
not god's blood
but the nomad's

our wanderings
on this mountain
measured in footsteps
buffered &
uploaded

21.22

on the uber ride
back from the airport
I see, for the first time in
almost a year, still working her same
corner at city park & canal,
sister natalie, or whatever
her name is today, and I think
to repeat my "alms-deeds" and
catch up, for maybe it is indeed
true that "he who has not amended his ways,
but yet has intermingled his profligate and
wicked actions with works of mercy,
shall receive mercy in the judgment"
but the traffic is constant
and we press on

21.23

it would be "the height of absurdity"
to suggest "the eternal life of the saints"
be anything less than endless or
that the endless punishment of
everyone else last even a moment less,
just as the bourgeois lifetime of ease
matches the lifelong struggle of the rabble,
the authority of the master mirrors
the subservience of the slave,
the intelligence of the scholar
contrasts to the ignorance of his detractors,
or the legal privilege of the male
mirrors the subordination of the female
in holy matrimony

21.24

our new governor elect landry tells
tucker carlson he'll turn
new orleans into a city of
the godly, especially those
god-fearing enough to make
six-figure donations to his cause
(i.e. himself), boysie bollinger
is high bidder to chair
the committee to divy up
the spoils, so we'll soon see
which christian gets which
zip code

21.25

"...what it is in reality, and not sacramentally,
to eat his body and drink his blood..."

not, that is, the *sacramentum,* or
'oath of obedience and fidelity
taken by roman soldiers on enlistment,
or the sum which two parties to a suit
first deposit, a cause, a civil suit...'

but the eating
and the drinking for sheer
sensual delight

21.26

"...god forbid that this love should be consumed
as wood, hay, stubble, and not rather be reckoned
a structure of gold, silver, precious stones..."

god forbid, indeed, though when
humans have need of fire they
burn whatever is at hand

& a haze of woodsmoke hangs

over the tent city
as the garbage detail begins its sweep

21.27

but since even the "bountiful
almsgiving" of those whose
time is worth a penny
a click wouldn't be enough
to provide a tenth of these
profligate souls "eternal habitation"
(though who *truly* believes
in eternal life anyway?)
is there really any need to keep
reaching in my pocket for quarters
and rolling down the window
in the piss stench?

22.00

a city—
what we call a city—
city of glass,
city of infusion,
city of yellow letters
reflected in
car windows,
city of the one-
armed beggar,
of wet cigarettes &
needles in the gutter,
this nomad tribe
lost in a desert,
mote in a pile of
dead leaves
heaped on the sidewalk

22.01

ultrasound reveals:
triplets!

(a second blasto appeared as
the first one split, 2 identi-
cals and a fraternal)
jacqui's terrified & we
for her

this trinity trusses meaning—
father makes son by bi-
furcation, holy
ghost by a-
doption, & we
are tied tightly

three dots on the banner
of the anthropocene

allegory of the
one in three,
the one who can
finally see
itself
on the family tree

22.02

though sometimes the
allegory un-
hitches from its
moral and drifts
for the sheer
joy of the sojourn

peregrine, your journey's
almost over & all you wish
for are these poor-
ly painted scenes

that hippie—pete,
his name was—came down
from the mountain and stood in

line at the post office where
mike's mom was working
the window that day, and
when he drew a sleepy
hand through his beard
a caterpillar fell out
on the counter

22.03

the crucifixion of george santos

o "god whom the pagan
deities tremble before,"
your ninety-plus-rated wine
tastes like vinegar
on my botox'd lips

my party my party why
hast thou forsaken me?
(just wait till I'm res-
urrected you'll be sorry)

so many of our colleagues
fixated on the cross, meta-
phorically speaking, enduring unto
truth, like pagan ordeal

but the *große lüge*
can't be nailed down
along the twin axes
of the two sexes

metaphor the original,
the antediluvian, lie?
lie we can't live
without? like

22.04

that bodies like ours may rise
up to heaven should surprise
us no more than spirits like theirs
coming down to animate flesh, he
argues to his old mentor
cicero, for how could we enjoy
heaven without a body to feel
the joy, happy ending
to the long story
of our life on earth?

history plausible to the
point of certainty points
to a certain future,
distracts
from the mystic con-
templation of the present moment
(twitter of bird feet
on the tin roof, or a
distant train whistle) where
the actual god
might actually wait

crack the language
like an egg &
today falls out

that bodies like
ours may rise

22.05

"the three incredibles"

she's walking down the median &
I'm thinking she might faint the way
she weaves and stumbles, eyes
rolled back, talking to the air

like some sibyl, but seems to regain
consciousness when she gets
to my window & takes my five-spot

'god bless you god bless what are
your names? well god bless you bill &
nick I'm sister natalie & I'll pray for you'

she crosses herself then brings her one
hand to prayer position

'dear god thank you for bill & nick bless
them as they go through their day
doing your work amen'

she has her t-shirt hiked up
over her midriff on this
warm december day,
belly pooching out...

is she pregnant?

22.06

december 2023

republicans agree to back ukraine
so long as the razor wire is
reinforced on the mexican border,
for to allow alleviation
of suffering on one front they
demand it be redoubled on another
(to keep the prophecy true)

likewise the gospel ai aims
israeli guns at three of their
own, waving white flags no less,
& mows them down, to balance
the calls for cease-fire inside
their own borders, for

equity is the rule
of engagement when
the god of moses and
the god of mohammed
square off

cicero may say "no war is
to be undertaken save for safety
or for honour" but in our
world, like the saguntines',
danger and dishonour
balance out the ledgers

22.07

augustine's argument for christ's
resurrection resembles trump's
for election fraud, i.e. how could
something so blatantly ridiculous
be believed by so many, in an age
as sublimely enlightened as ours,
except the knowledge be imparted
divinely ('I know I just know,'
'I can feel it') and then
"fertilized richly with the
blood of the martyrs"

22.08

in milan a blind man's sight
was restored by proximity
to the martyrs; in carthage
innocentia cured her breast
cancer with prayer; likewise
in carthage, a "gouty doctor," beset
by "black woolly-haired boys"
who prevented him being washed
in the "laver of regeneration,"
dove in anyway and cast off
both the boys and the gout;

in victoriana a young lad's
eyeball hung by a thread
but when he popped it back in
was perfectly fine; & there was
the strange case of the
man with six rectal
fistulæ of which five were repaired
by surgery but when the doctor
drew out his knife to cure the sixth
he could find it neither
by sight nor by palpation
with his finger

this is not to mention the poor fellow
who needed a coat and found a fish
with a gold ring inside it, which bought
him enough wool for his wife to sew,
nor the brother and sister who came
to augustine's sermon and lost the shakes
their evil mother had given them with a spell

indeed the miracles, what we call signs,
continue in our own enlightened time,
when at the pentecostal holiness church
twenty at once were seized
by the spirit and praised
him in tongues heretofore
unheard by human ears, and in
alabama the faithful caress
deadly venomous serpents
and are not bitten

22.09

jan 9, 2024

ultrasonic gender reveal:
two girls cuddling
together in their sack,
and the fraternal one

off to the side, a sequestration
he will remember,
I imagine, at
certain moments

at the other end of life my own
internal imaging:
random memories,
a word, complete
with tone & inflection,
my mother spoke
six decades ago
(*'pungent'*) lights up
beside that image of
the beggar on the curb
from yesterday (jacket of black
fleece right arm extended
for alms left sleeve
hanging empty slight
bulge at the belly)

the saint, of like age,
confessed similar distractions
in his youth, but now must
focus his attention
on the vandals at the gate
(for philosophers and clerics,
soldiers and sailors,
shepherds, bakers,
carpenters and scribes...
every swingin' dick
is called to the parapet now)

& if they fall they fall
as a martyr falls
"...conquering the world
not by resisting it, but by dying"

22.10

the saint says "...demons wrought these
marvels with the same impure pride
with which they aspired to be
the gods of the nations..."

gods on either side of the
ukraine line today, fixed in a
frozen landscape that looks more
like w.w.i. than iii, all but forgotten
in the hoopla around netan-
yahu's bid to rewrite history (this time
actually erasing the seed of amalek)
and the i.c.j. scratching its head
over whether the annihilation
of a race constitutes genocide
and houthis taking pot shots at 'our'
freighters, various 'iran proxies' lobbing
missiles and drones, even killing three
americans (biden watching solemnly,
saluting in silence but scowling as
loud as he can, as the three caskets
are unloaded from the c-130 on this
gray drizzly day in january 2024)
and they're gathering at the borders in
texas and iran to call on whichever son
of abram to rain fire and brimstone
on whoever dropped it on them last night,
whether jesus rides the missile like
slim pickens in dr. strangelove or
imageless mohammed pilots the drone,
the souls rise like concepts out of the con-
crete, bodies broken in the rubble

22.11

"what does this soul, which is
finer than all else, do in such
a mass of matter as this?"

this mardi gras
I go as a mystic
starfish, mouth
pressed to your
bottom, breathing in
saltwater &
bits of sand

the current
moves through me
ferociously
& then through thee
& then subsides

ever repentant we
imagine doing it
more frequently
& then don't

everyone gives up
something for lent, ex-
changing beef for fried
fish on friday, for example,
swearing off booze
or drugs or whatever gave
pleasure to this city
of the fallen,
and we do also, we
pagans, not from faith
but its utter lack,
bowing to the kitsch since
there is nothing else

on n.p.r. an old
man remembers
his first time
looking down on
a priest's bald head
as it licked his hairless

member, mumbling in latin,
its lesson handed down
through generations

'I would have
sold cocaine
on the streetcorner,'
said the preacher,
'if jesus hadn't found me'

22.12

"...their way is to... cast ridicule on our faith
in the resurrection of the body by asking
whether abortions shall rise..."

and should this question extend
to the frozen embryos that
nurse in alabama dropped,
murdered, or
her boss did, by letting
her handle them?

it falls to the impartial
courts to decide by ordeal
when life and murder begin
(shareholders hold your breath)

gov. landry does what he can,
making concealed carry man-
datory, resurrecting the electric
chair to protect the
right to life

sister natalie (did her belly
shrink?) appears at my window,
oversized t-shirt pulled off
her left shoulder
to expose the stump, with its
cardboard sign tucked under,

anything helps god bless,
stands staring at me
but I don't roll down

22.13

'lust for life'

my teeth are fantastic,
the hygienist says,
& she recognizes
my ring tone, which
makes me smile

later I take the dog
for a walk in the woods
of city park, puffing the vape
as I go, until I notice
I am lost

at a broken picnic table
forgotten in a thicket
I sit on the bench and
study the forest floor,
oak leaves like a cast of runes,
debris of a long-dead language
or shards of a fallen
citadel, signifying system
reduced to mulch

I get up and head back
to the truck, walk for ten
minutes and come to that
table again, & time and place,
north, south, left, right
reverse in the mind like a
sail coming about

will I die in this bewildered state,
entranced by dead letters on the ground?

the dog lies among them, panting,
one eye on me

the bayou was on my left as I walked out
and is on my left again as I head back, for
in dementia as in nietzsche we
return, but with a difference

for I had never imagined her,
in her surgical mask and
scrubs, an old punk like me

22.14

israel initiates a
thorough & transparent
hallucination-free invest-
igation of the seven world
kitchen workers inter-
cepted bringing loaves
& fishes to gaza, taken
out by drone strike when
an i.d.f. mistook a spat-
ula for an a.r., but then
ben n. finally
bends, lets in
seven trucks
of fish meal and flour as
trade for biden not cutting
his own a.r. supply

here it rains hard all day,
underpasses swamping
toyota after toyota,
& at an open man-
hole on orleans
where muddy water spins
down like a tub drain
into the abyss below,

some guy knee-
deep in it looking
down into the vortex,
current tearing at his legs—
I yell at him to get away
but he is hypnotized

22.15

the triplets

21 folk in gowns and masks it
takes to bring this tri-
nity into the cold
light of the o.r., two months
early, claude the big guy at
4 pounds 3, freya at 3, and little ada
just over 2, pics on whatsapp
of the tiny larval forms in a blue-
gloved hand and later in n.i.c.u. boxes
tangled among their tubes
and sensors, on webcam

& on this day one
is born in gaza at 7 months,
pulled from the dead mother
at a bomb site, video of the
doctor who happened to be there
running through the wrecked city,
infant under his arm like a football wrapped
in a keffiyeh, to the bombed out
hospital where they manage to
get it breathing and named,
grandparents at the incubator
weeping for their lost children,
steeling themselves with a votive
pledge this child will pass on to its own

should any of these children perish,
augustine maintains,

"...when the general resur-
rection shall have arrived..."
they shall stand as tall as christ did
when he appeared to the disciples, in
"the bloom of youth
at about the age of thirty"

hard to believe looking at ada's
thigh the size of my index finger,
but on this point, he says, "the world's
wisest men agree"

22.16

another delicious
meal on the porch–
you are what you eat said tiny
tiny tim, in which case I
must be pretty yummy,
our ancient references
whether to him or some
defunct cartoon or to an old
half-fantasized saint
are private language, not mutually
intelligible with these natural signs
of the city, gunshots & sirens &
distant trumpets—
we talk through the quick
bursts, both of us feeling
better since we gave up
meat, mostly anyway, and
booze, mostly anyway, and I'd
rather be hearing your
talk & seeing your face across
the table on the back porch
by multicolored l.e.d.'s than
most anything, including even
those moments I owe entirely
to you, the souks in marrakech
for example, or sheepdog trials

in the shetlands, or walking the cliff
at duino, or stumbling upon cubanismo
on the opatija boardwalk,
or seeing dylan one last time, or lucinda,
or a night out in prague when that gray-
blue sky spun overhead, or
swimming naked in asturias,
or blowing a tire in the lake country,
or hanging in the bar next door, or any thing or
body else that isn't you, back on our
porch in this city of dying gods, nanc,
mi luz, mi vida, mi corazon, mi tulipán

22.17

5/5/24, the brain-worm

the brain-worm
in the nation's cranium
is confused,
self-diagnosing its dysphoria &
paranoid phantasies,
hallucinations of self
excreted by the
munching parasite, but
after the general resurrection
says augustine
clarity shall reign—
"there shall be no lust,
which is now the cause of
confusion"—and all of
us shall be resurrected
with bodies of strapping
30-year-olds, like christ
upon ascension, & even aborted
fetuses, even the deformed, the
retarded, even amputees and
those burned alive, even
decrepit old beggars like
me and sister natalie,

all shall rise in the vigor
of young manhood...
and to resolve a certain
confusion
among colleagues
& competitors aug-
gustine adds, "the female
members shall remain,
adapted not to the old
uses but to a new beauty,"
leaving no doubt that
women shall rise as wo-
men (& fit for new use!)
not as men like
us, and just as
we men & we wo-
men shall be resurrected
from our cthonic final
place, the brain-worm
shall rise from the dark
cave of the mortal
mind to become a radiant
halo lighting the face of its
ultra-handsome host

22.18

"...understanding both sexes to be
included under the general term 'man'?"

etymology of a feeling:

re-
membering *mems-ro,*
'queasy innards'
at the dawn of the west,
that feeling half
terror half giddy
delight manwoman felt
deep in her member,

in the pit of her
stomach,
like young
lovers do
(& old guys too),
or hagar on her mission,
abram awaiting,
sarai watching
from the wing,
stage fright
in the bedroom, blushing
& trembling, or riding
to first grade
telling my mother my
stomach hurt and she
said I was just worried,
and I guess I was,
worried
what would happen
when I got to school
or when I started work or when I
go through the hospital doors
for the last time
I was
a bird among
these spirits, fledgling
floating in a pond
like the brown thrasher I
found that summer—we
nursed it with an eyedropper
till it learned to eat &
one day it sat
on my mother's
shoulder at the dinner table
and every time she
raised her fork
opened its mouth

22.19

"what am I to say now
about the hair and nails?"

in my dream my friends
appear in their youth, thin
and pretty like forty years ago—
I realize I'm dreaming and try
to tell them they aren't making
out by the fire in the backyard
but having their fun in my
dream, but they're too
engrossed in each other to
listen, and go
back to kissing

likewise augustine's warnings
ring out unheeded
and we go on making
love and money in this
world he is dreaming

my dream re-
vealed to me
that my friends were
lovers, back in the day,
and kept it secret—
likewise the saint
questions his dream
for the secret history it reveals
and the future it augurs,
and feels the sting
of our deception

22.20

on this sweltering
summer day,
asphalt bubbling

under her flip-flops,
she steps up to my
window &
I see my shot:

'would you mind
if I took your
picture? it's for
a book I'm writing?'

'oh suuuure' she says and
poses exuberantly,
bouncing her cardboard
sign like a pompom
in the one hand and
waving the stump around
in a little dance as if
to summon
the lost arm
to fly from wherever
it may have fallen,
on land or in the sea
or in primordial
pools of molten lava,
back onto her body
to make it whole
again

"for in the resurrection of the flesh
the body… shall enjoy the beauty
that arises from preserving symmetry
and proportion in all its members"

22.21

"[the] law in his members warring
against the… law of his mind…"
was it? simple enough
if you're ambivalent about
going out tonight, more complicated

if you're putting extinction of the species
on the table, biden thinking he's the only
one who can stand up to *il duce*, for
example (the slightest lapse of
rhetoric and you want me to stand
down? never will I give up fighting
for the divan on air force one!)—

meanwhile trump manages to
get slightly martyred, then with
stylishly bandaged ear
prays at the
podium for unity (at
least among those who
can afford pornstars)
and biden stumbles on
with his lance high
for about five minutes
before passing the bur-
den of proof to kamala,
causing everyone, quite despite
ourselves, to feel a glimmer, as we
"do our best to conjecture
the great glory of that state
which we cannot worthily
speak of, because we have
not yet experienced it,"
and who'll get the honor,
this time, of sacking
their own capital and
blaming the other's god?

22.22

to believe the great lie
is to be the true mystic, holy
one who sees through reality
to the real of pure desire

"this life itself, if
life it is to be called," he says,
attests to this eternal verity
with its litany of temporal miseries

that is to say, the fall
is in the naming, belief
the shark fin of doubt,
the more he believes the
less belief he owns &
the more the rhetoric
glows—
he orders the amanuensis to
expand the catalog,
strike the conjunctions or unfurl poly-
syndeton, pleonasm, conceits
that wind like a dragonfly's path,
metonymies to take
the breath away, symbols
that send a
shiver up the spine

so we may know
beyond the shadow

22.23

28 august (augustine's death day / feast day), 2024

"...lest a semblance of truth deceive us,
lest a subtle discourse blind us..."

I recall on you
that 'old man smell'
that clings to me now, sweat and
sawdust and coffee, forearms
brown with purple bruises
below the folded sleeve but
undersides pale as a lizard's belly,
the hand that grips my shoulder

thickly calloused, serrated almost,
half-forgotten memories
activated by the smell of my-
self, your pith helmet and khakis,
'engineer boots'—when I was
four I threw the sllen
wrenches in the pond and you
whipped me for it, and though
I've crossed a world since then
that day set my course.

a smell hangs over the ancient
body politic, too—the stench of rat piss
closed city hall today.
where is it coming from?
what specific office?
what sordid life teems
in the spaces between rooms, in the wall
cavities, plumbing pits & raceways?
what species thrives in this darkness,
eating shit and each other,
drinking from the sewer stream?

likewise we sniff
emanations from our old language
which, now in its decrepitude,
still strains and stumbles like
a war-horse under its burden
of weapons and ambition.
I can feel the heat and smell
the sweat through these
synaesthetic syllables.

you were solid
hard, angular, scary
like it would hurt
to run into you, but
then came the stink,
and you went soft and
weak as a kitten,

having to lean on me or
my mother just to shuffle
from the bed to the recliner,
where, december
19, 1997, you breathed
your last soft sigh.

22.24

the "rich and
countless blessings" of
"his retributive justice":
orgasm on the deathbed, mystic
erotic asphyxiation, since
"those who copulate
can generate nothing," i.e.
connoisseurs only at this
mar-a-lago of the mind,
no breeders allowed
'ooooo I love black men...
black women not
so much' brags
trump at the rally—mental
tease to intensify
sensation

22.25

"...as it was also predicted that the world would believe,
a prediction not due to the sorceries of peter (vide 18.53)"

as that 'floating island of garbage' the trump campaign
girds its loins for the final week before
erection day (trump winking to mike johnson,
sharing a little secret, maybe the new plan to fight
global warming by dismantling n.o.a.a.) &
the city brings in state cops and
wildlife and fisheries to liquidate
the tent city under the freeway &
avert distraction of the rich white girls

(700 m. total economic impact!)
following taylor swift to the dome,
a 'mass movement of joy,'
(they say tayl donated thousands of styrofoam
meal plates to the newly 'homeless')
"spiritual felicity," dopamine crowd surf
and everyone looks just like you

22.26

5 november, election day—

we watched an episode
of something we immediately forgot,
then turned off the t.v.

"...they shall never lose [their bodies]
even for the briefest moment,
nor ever lay them down in death..."

eros as the turning away, sickened,
from porphyry and plato's for-
ensic arguments, for

democracy is kingdom of
desire, pleasure in bondage,
hideous orange face on the flag—

morning after, at city park & canal
a guy slouches shirtless on the
bench next to a heap of filthy bedding

sister natalie appears through a crack
in the cemetery wall, lights a cigarette
on the windless day

we're stunned but not truly surprised,
having secretly felt its inevitability, & now
relieved we no longer have to pretend

don't leave love out of
the equation, mark told me, but this
might be something I'm not equal to

augustine, too, speaks of love,
of using love to drive
the vandals from the gate

caritas, for example, of 'conservative causes'
bernie marcus leaves his billions to, charity
of 'calling that woke crap what it is'

& as trump assembles his 'cabinet'
who's rubbing their palms?
or does it really matter which

fungible token sits at which office
depot desk? like those n. korean soldiers
tanking into a ukraine they've never heard of

drones on the front line, orders from
the a.i., and after the battle those still
living returned to their benches

22.27

plato plus porphyry, augustine argues,
pretty much equal a christian, as
"both of them would readily concede,
that if the souls of the saints are to be
reunited to bodies, it shall be
to their own bodies," not
to some random body they
find on the street (imagine
the chaos that would reign
in a city where souls pop in and
out of bodies at will, how could
lovers and friends, family and
police keep track?) &
we can imagine

that the souls of saints will
have no problem discerning
from the realm of bodiless bliss
just which of those number-
less bodies is "their own"
so it wouldn't be possible for, say,
plato's soul to enter sister natalie's
body by mistake, nor for sister natalie
to wake up one day inside her
neighbor on the bench, nor
for any wandering soul to find
its own body occupied by
someone else (like porphyry) when
it returns from its sojourn, at least
we can say such corporal con-
fusion would be extremely rare,
not at all the normal case, for

22.28

unlike language which moves
freely mouth to mouth, souls
are not profligate but true
to their bodies as the bride
to her husband,
though in this passage (as
in many) it does rather
sound like augustine porphyry
cicero varro plato labeo and
the gang having an
evening in the back room
of the bourbon pub
where essences discourse
as freely among the bodies
as augustine's philosophers,
souls of disparate ages,
commingle in the text, like-
wise the friendly flow of capital
between members at mar
a lago is its own little parable

of resurrection, in which multi-
ple souls combine wits to re-
invigorate the moldy corpses
of great tyrants of the past to
"receive bodies in which they may live
eternally without suffering" &
"the whole question of the eternal
resurrection of the body shall be
resolved out of their own mouths"

22.29

of the beatific vision

after all
is said and
done, after
the rise and after
the fall, after all
the voices cease
to echo in the hall,
after the big bang,
after the flood,
after the last
wildfire, the great
conflagration,
after christ has come
again, and gone,
after all have been
judged and found
wanting or pure,
after that before which
was no after and
after which will be no
before, after all
who spoke
no longer speak
and all who were mute
are mute no more,
after we have let go

our physical bodies and
stand clothed in light, in
perfect immortal frame,
without employment nor
need of it, then we will
finally see this famous god,
the physical god,
though not, if we
may clarify, with these
physical eyes,
not with eyes
of green or black or
blue, not with eyes
that may be
open or closed, or
blurred or clear,
not with eyes that
may look and then
look away, that may half
close in tiredness or desire,
or shift their attention
from without to within,
or be distracted
by a fleeting shadow
of imagined enemy or
friend, but eyes which see
as through a glass
darkly, eyes which
though they be
closed, still see,
& though our view
be blocked
by fortress wall
or parapet
we shall still see
the great valley,
the looming mountain,
and in the shadow
of that mountain
in the hollow

of that valley
a lone horseman
coming across the plain
like a speck on the mountain
like a mote in the valley
steadfast as an ant
it comes
down into the dark and back
up the other side
through farmland and
villages and the ruins
of great estates,
hooves on grass &
then on cobblestone
finally on marble
through the gate
down the passageway
up the stair
into the tower
until the horse
stands before me,
nostrils flaring,
stomping its feet,
and the rider—
the rider is a knight,
or sometimes I think
a cowboy, or
then again sometimes,
perhaps even now,
I think the rider is
st. joan—
hands me a purse,
a purse of fine
suede, the softest
leather you have ever
touched, and inside,
I can feel them, the
five hexagonal shafts,
each with a short
90 degree bend

22.30

1/6/25, election certification day, four years since 1.1

"eternal felicity,"
feel of the city,
copping a feel
from the city

for the force
isis insists
that through
the fresh
flesh drives
the rented ford
is is, insists

as I wake I am
climbing a ladder,
all the way to the third
floor of this ram-
shackle house,
hanging on to
the cornice as
the piece-of-shit ladder (broken
rungs bolstered with
scraps of 2x4) sways
under me, and I
am terrified—
but the others are
already up there, having simply
taken the stairs

"in that blessed city
there shall be
this great blessing,
that no inferior shall envy
any superior"

sister natalie, in fleece
jacket with the empty
sleeve, with her card-
board sign, sporting a
goatee today,
seems o.k.,
not babbling or chanting as
she sometimes does but
business-like,
ducking into the bus stop
out of the wind
to light a cig

kamala reads the pro-
nouncement—
dogs on pedestals
stand on hind legs

twelfth night:
la passion de jeanne d'arc rolls
through the quarter—
joan is
a friend of ours &
hands us a handful
of chocolate doubloons

"one thing is certain, the body
shall forthwith be wherever
the spirit wills"

I keep forgetting
who's still living
& who's already dead
& how we
tell them apart
like we tell
dream & waking a-
part or
thought & speaking
word & image

dance & dancing
bush & burning—
flow of all things
that can no
longer be told
a part

what's to come?
the siege, the slow
battle we won't see
the end of?

fossil exhibit
at the museum of
natural history?

yet more slaughter?

this city I leave
to my trinity, my
two trinities, this
world to the rest of you,
evermore

glossary

A partial list of names and more esoteric terms encountered in the poems.

Adeodatus. Augustine's son by his unnamed concubine. Referred to by Augustine, alternately, as "gift from god" (the meaning of his name) and "the product of my sin," the boy is reported in Catholic lore to have been brilliant. When Augustine split, after fifteen years, with his lover, Adeodatus stayed with his father and joined him in his conversion to Christianity in 387, when the two were baptized in a single ceremony performed by St. Ambrose. Augustine was in his 30s at this time, the boy 15. The boy died only a year later, of unrecorded causes.

Alaric. Warrior king who led the Visigoths in the sacking of Rome in 410. Once an ally of Rome under Theodosius, Alaric helped defeat the Franks and other would-be rebels, losing thousands of his troops in the process, but he received little recognition from Rome for his sacrifice and left the Roman army enraged. After the death of Theodosius, as the Roman armies began to disintegrate in 395, he became king of the Visigoths and turned against the weakened Romans, finally sacking Rome in 410. After this victory, however, the Visigoths left the ravaged city, having no desire to administer an empire.

Alignments. See Carnac Alignments, below.

Amalek, seed of (22.10 and elsewhere). Amalek and the Amalekites are referred to repeatedly in the Hebrew Bible as enemies of Israel. Among many other references, in Deuteronomy 7:1–16 and Deuteronomy 25:16–18 the Jews are commanded to utterly destroy the Amalekites, their bloodline and their livestock, and in 1 Samuel 15 it is reported that King Saul loses favor with Yahweh for failing in this task. In modern Israel, Palestinians are sometimes referred to as "the seed of Amalek" by hawkish soldiers and politicians, including Netanyahu himself, who used the phrase after the Hamas attack on Israel in October 2023 leading up to the invasion of Gaza: "You must remember what Amalek has done to you, says our Holy Bible," he said in the broadcast, "and we do remember." When South Africa brought the charge of genocide to the International Court of Justice, part of their evidence was video footage of Israeli soldiers chanting, "Wipe out the seed of Amalek."

Apuleius (8.16 and elsewhere). Second century Numidian philosopher, author of, most famously, *The Golden Ass* (a.k.a. *The Metamorphoses*) who, like Augustine a century later, began his studies at Carthage and later became a devoted Platonist. Unlike Augustine, however, Apuleius retained his Platonism and was an initiate into several mystery cults, including the Dionysian. Augustine attacks, at some length, here, Apuleius's *De Deo Socratis (On the God of Socrates)*, which was an examination of the behavior of demons and a work which would certainly have drifted into obscurity (the original text was ordered to be burned by Theodosius) had not Augustine made it famous by devoting multiple chapters of *City of God* to its refutation.

Atys. The Phrygian demon Agdistis originally had both male and female sex organs, but this frightened the Olympian gods who cut off the male member and tossed it away. It grew into an almond tree, and the young goddess Nana put one of the nuts in her bosom, which caused her to become pregnant with Atys. Agdistis' female half, Cybele, fell in love with Atys (even though, or perhaps because, she was also his father) and revealed herself in all her splendor, which frightened young Atys into castrating himself.

Carlson, Tucker. Tucker Swanson McNear Carlson (b. 1969), American television host and conservative political commentator who has hosted the nightly political talk show *Tucker Carlson Tonight* on Fox News since 2016, tireless advocate of Trumpian conspiracy theories, sometimes even criticizing Trump for not being Trump enough.

Carnac Alignments. Groupings of *menhirs*, or standing stones, that are considered to be the oldest surviving human-made structure in Europe, the oldest of them dating to 4900 BCE, considerably older than Stonehenge. They stand in and around Carnac, France, on the Brittany coast. In the early modern era a legend circulated that when the Romans invaded the region Merlin turned the soldiers into stones, which is why they stand in regimented formation.

Casey (16.20). Wife of Desantis, Ron (q.v. below).

glossary

Cato. Marcus Porcius Cato (95–46 BCE), a.k.a. Cato the Younger, was a conservative Roman senator in the period of the late republic who vehemently opposed Julius Caesar. Known for his immunity to bribes and staunch opposition to the general corruption of the period, he killed himself upon Caesar's rise to the throne rather than serve under him, though he encouraged his son to be prudent and submit to the new regime.

Cicero. Marcus Tullius Cicero (106–43 BCE), Roman statesman, lawyer, scholar, philosopher and Academic Skeptic. His treatises on rhetoric, philosophy and politics, were and are still vastly influential and would have been a central pillar of Augustine's education.

The Council of Rome. ("council," 1.09) a meeting, 382 AD, of Catholic Church officials and theologians in which certain foundational issues (the biblical canon, the divinity of Christ, etc.) were decided by vote.

The Cuman Apollo (3.11). The Apollonian oracle at Cumae, the ancient Greek colony located near Naples, was assigned great importance in early Rome—greater than any other oracle—by Virgil (*Aeneid* VI) because of its proximity to the City. The statue of Apollo there was said to have wept for four days during a battle with the Greeks, but attempts by various augurs and soothsayers to interpret the tears were inconclusive, and the decision was made to throw it into the sea to quiet the weeping.

Cybele. A mystery goddess to the Greeks, protector of Athens, who through some subtle twists in her mythography became in Roman tradition the Mother of the Gods.

Darrow, Clarence. See "Scopes Trial," below.

Desantis, Ron. In 2023, governor of Florida and challenger to Trump for the Republican presidential nomination. Famous for, among other things, state takeovers of colleges and schools to replace faculty and staff with conservative hacks. He loved to say, "Florida is where woke comes to die."

Dods. Marcus Dods editor/translator of the 1872 English edition of *The City of God*, the primary text consulted for this work.

glossary

Donatists (2.16 and elsewhere). Donatism was a Christian sect rooted in the Roman province of Africa Proconsularis (present-day Tunisia, near Augustine's see in old Hippo). Founded by the Berber Christian bishop Donatus Magnus, and practiced mainly among the indigenous Berber population, the sect successfully blended Christianity with local Berber customs. This made it unpopular with the Roman church and especially with Augustine, who frequently rails against it in spite or perhaps because of his own suppressed Berber heritage.

Eleusis. This site of the worship of Demeter and Persephone, or the Eleusinian Mysteries, was considered among the most sacred of ancient Greece.

Enoch. Antediluvian figure in the Hebrew Bible, son of Jared and father of Methuselah. Genesis 5:24 reports that Enoch "walked with God: and he was no more; for God took him," which is interpreted by Augustine and some other Jewish and Christian scholars as meaning that Enoch entered heaven without having to die first. Augustine (in 15.10) uses the term "translation" (*translatus*) to describe this process. See also "Septuagint Scandal" below.

Essentia. From root *esse* ("to be"), present active infinitive of *sum* ("I am"), a term coined by Cicero to translate Ancient Greek οὐσία (*ousía*), from Greek philosophy, where it means substance or essence, the nature of a thing that makes it a member of a class. Also, more colloquially, that which one owns, property (in both senses of the word). Over history the word acquired esoteric implications: in alchemy, a fire-resistant substance; in magic, a material thing which connects a person and a spirit, a voodoo doll, for example.

"Eudemons" online (https://www.eudemons.com/) is a contemporary role-playing game which takes its name from a concept of classical philosophy. Augustine uses the word in 9.13 to refer to "good demons," (in contrast to cacodemons, which would be "bad demons"), in a quiet reference to Aristotle, for whom, in the *Nicomachean Ethics*, *eudaimonia* (which might translate to "living well" or "well-being" or, as Augustine uses it here, "blessedness") became a central concept alongside contrasting terms such as *aretē* (usually translated as "virtue") and *phronesis* ("practical or ethical wisdom").

Eugenius. Flavius Eugenius (d. 394) was a usurper in the Western Roman Empire (392–394) against Emperor

Theodosius I. Though (theoretically) Christian himself, Eugenius capitalized on the discontent caused by Theodosius' targeting of pagans, restoring rites and temples and reviving the pagan cause. He was captured and executed by Theodosius at the Battle of Frigidus.

Falwell, Jerry (Sr. and Jr.). Jerry Laymon Falwell Sr. (1933–2007), Baptist pastor, televangelist, conservative activist, founder of the "Moral Majority" PAC in 1979. His Thomas Road Baptist Church, a megachurch in Lynchburg, Virginia, evolved into the Lynchburg Christian Academy and finally into Liberty University in 1971. Upon his death he ceded Liberty University to his son, Jerry Falwell Jr. (1962-). After leading the university to financial success, with (in 2020) 15k students on campus and 80k online, Jr. was shunted out of the office for a variety of financial shenanigans, as well as the scandal around the revelation that he regularly watched his wife Becki having sex with a lover in their employ.

Faustus the Manichæan, more usually known as Faustus of Mileve, was a Manichaean bishop of the fourth century, now remembered only for his encounter with Augustine in Carthage around 383, which Augustine recounts in the *Confessions*. Augustine, during his brief tenure as a Manichee, sought him out as a teacher, later rebuking him in both the *Confessions* and a later, more vehement, treatise, *Contra Faustum*.

Fimbria. Gaius Flavius Fimbria, according to Cicero, became a consul in 104 BCE. Cicero describes him as a clever jurist and formidable orator, though bitter and vehement in speaking, and Augustine describes him (in 3.07) only as "the veriest villain," responsible for the sacking of Ilium.

Francis, Norman. Norman C. Francis (1931–), African-American academic, president of Xavier University of Louisiana from 1968-2015. During the "take 'em down" movement, the name of Jefferson Davis Parkway in New Orleans was changed to Norman C Francis Parkway.

Frenchmen Street. A New Orleans street, just outside the French Quarter in Faubourg Marigny, which has come to almost surpass Bourbon Street in both popularity and the frenzy of available debaucheries.

glossary

Goose (cackling of the) (3.08). In Augustine's day, geese were sometimes caged at the gates of the city because they would raise alarms by cackling loudly at the approach of strangers.

große lüge (pl. großen lügen). German expression (literally, "great lie") made famous by Adolf Hitler in *Mein Kampf*, to describe a lie so blatant that it had to be believed, for no one would dare make a statement so easily disproved, were it not the case.

Hagar. See "Sarah," below.

Heraclitus. Greek philosopher, c. 500 BCE, from Ephesus, is not specifically addressed in Paul's epistle to the Ephesians as I imply in 15.06, yet it seems he could have been, thus my synecdoche.

Hermes Trismegistus. Hermes the "thrice great," the early classical syncresis of the Greek Hermes and Egyptian Thoth, held, according to Augustine at least, that there were two types of gods, those created by the celestial God, and those created by man in the act of making their statues. However Augustine also sees in the hermetic writings a prediction of the rise of Christianity and so affords Hermes, like Plato, a certain reverence as an enlightened pagan voice, one of the harbingers of the *prisca theologia,* the single, true theology that threads through all religions. "Hermes... seems to predict the present time, in which the Christian religion is overthrowing all lying figments with a vehemence and liberty proportioned to its superior truth and holiness...." (8.23)

Hydromorphone. A potent schedule II opioid drug, "synthetic heroin," often called on the street by its best-known brand name, Dilaudid.

Ilium. The ancient mytho-historical city of Troy, in modern-day Turkey, was sieged and sacked in 85 BCE, for no apparent reason, by Fimbria, q.v.

Imperium, jus imperium. In Roman law the *jus imperium* (from the Latin *imperare,* to command, same root as "emperor") designated the right of command and punishment for any citizen over their inferiors, a right not only to enforce the law but on occasion to modify it, and to enact immediate (i.e. in the street) punishment.

jemaa el-fna. The great and ancient plaza at the center of old Marrakesh.

Johnson, Mike. Louisiana congressman, famous for his 'Christian Nationalism,' questioning the efficacy of separation of church and state and advocating instead for a state in service to the church, much like the Rome of Augustine's day. Johnson was elected Speaker of the House of Representatives of the United States in October 2023.

Kat Von D, (7.16) tattoo artist to the stars, announced in October 2021 that she would be closing her Hollywood shop, High Voltage, and moving with her family to Indiana.

Kennedy, Handy. Handy Kennedy, contemporary African-American farmer in Georgia, founder of the AgriUnity cooperative, a group of Black farmers formed to better their chances of economic success and fight discriminatory practices of federal aid programs.

Laâbi. Abdellatif Laâbi (1942–) (8.04), Moroccan poet and activist, co-founder of the influential Francophone journal *Souffles* and its Arabic-language counterpart, *Anfas*, was tortured and imprisoned 1972-80 by the repressive Moroccan regime, then forced into exile in France, where he achieved literary notoriety, and was then welcomed back to Morocco as a hero.

Labeo. Dods's note on one of Augustine's more obscure references: "Labeo, a jurist of the time of Augustus, learned in law and antiquities, and the author of several works much prized by his own and some succeeding ages. The two articles in Smith's Dictionary on Antistius and Cornelius Labeo should be read."

Liber. A phallic god often closely associated or even confused with Bacchus. He was indeed worshiped with phallic rites, and his temples contained phallic imagery. The name, from which we derive that notion so seminal to colonial powers, "liberty," is of ancient, proto-Indo-European origin.

"licking a painted loaf." In 4.23 Augustine uses this expression to indicate the spiritual emptiness of worshiping pagan demons, i.e. one gets as much spiritual nourishment from them as one gets physical nourishment from licking a painting of a loaf of bread.

glossary

'love, and do what you will' (3.19 and elsewhere). One of Augustine's more famous quotes, from the *Homilies on the First Epistle of John*:

> Dilige, et quod vis fac: sive taceas, dilectione taceas; sive clames, dilectione clames; sive emendes, dilectione emendes; sive parcas, dilectione parcas: radix sit intus dilectionis, non potest de ista radice nisi bonum existere.
>
> (Love, and do what you will: whether you peace, through love hold your peace; whether you cry out, through love cry out; whether you correct, through love correct; whether you spare, through love do thou spare: let the root of love be within, from this root nothing but good can come into existence.)

Lucretia. According to Roman tradition, Lucretia was a noblewoman in ancient Rome (c. 500 BCE), who was raped by Sextus Tarquinius (Tarquin) and then committed suicide from the shame. Augustine (in 1.19 and elsewhere) meditates at length on the morality of this act (Lucretia's, not Tarquin's), which he terms a homicide.

Mahagonny. *Rise and Fall of the City of Mahagonny (Aufstieg und Fall der Stadt Mahagonny)*, the Brecht-Weill opera first performed in 1930, which tells the story of a city founded in vice, located obscurely on the gulf coast of the USA, which often sounds suspiciously like New Orleans.

Mamre, Oak of. Mamre is a site where Abraham pitched tents and built an altar (in Gen. 13:18) and was brought word from God, in the guise of three men, of Sarah's pregnancy (Gen. 18:1–15). In Genesis the site is described as 'the great trees of Mamre'. The reference to a single great tree, as opposed to a grove, appears to come from a discrepancy in the Septuagint translation (q.v.).

McCarthy, Kevin Owen (b.1965), American politician who won the 55th speaker of the United States House of Representatives election on January 7, 2023, after 14 failed attempts and a host of (public and also, certainly, private) concessions to the radical right in the Republican party, which unseated him a few months later and installed the even further right-leaning Louisiana congressman Mike Johnson (q.v.) in his place

Meloni, Giorgia. At time of writing, head of the neo-fascist Brothers of Italy (FDL) political party and Prime Minister of Italy.

mems-ro. (13.13 and 22.18) This is the standard lexical representation of the ancient Proto Indo-European root of the word *member,* the etymology of which is discussed in 13.13 and meditated on in 22.18. Dods uses *member* to translate Augustine's *membrum,* which appears in various declensions dozens of times in the text, especially toward the end. Augustine uses the term to mean a part of the body, often referring to genitalia (male or female), but also sometimes referring to other parts, such as, in 22.01, the eye: "...the eye is more excellent than the other members." The term acquired its contemporary meaning of a person belonging to a group or organization from the Biblical notion of the Church as the body of Christ; that is, to be a 'member of the church' is to be Christ's organ.

Numa. Numa Pompilius (753–673 BCE; reigned 715–673 BCE), legendary second king of Rome, after Romulus.

πᾰ́θος **(páthos)** n. pain, suffering, death, misfortune, calamity, disaster, misery, any strong feeling, passion, emotion, condition, state, incident, modification of words (Wiktionary).

Pear (pear thief, etc.). Mentions of pears or the pear thief herein refer to the famous passage in *The Confessions* in which Augustine confesses (or, arguably, brags) that when he was a child he stole pears from a neighbor's orchard, and he stole them not because he was hungry but simply because it was forbidden. In this anecdote he finds evidence of the Fall and humanity's innate wickedness.

Pickled punks. Carny term for abnormal (polycephalic, hermaphroditic, etc.) human fetuses preserved in jars of formaldehyde and used as sideshow attractions in circuses and traveling fairs, popular in the early 20th century. Imitation pickled punks— wax, rubber, plastic, etc.— are known as "bouncers" for their tendency to bounce when dropped.

Porphyry of Tyre (c. 234-305), Neoplatonic philosopher and late champion of pagan theology and theurgy. The fifteen books of his *Against the Christians* (Κατὰ Χριστιανῶν; *Adversus Christianos*) attracted rebuttals by some thirty Christian apologists, including (besides Augustine) Methodius, Eusebius, Apollinaris, and Jerome. All we know of Porphyry's arguments is found in these refutations, as in the fifth century Theodosius II ordered every copy of the text confiscated and burned.

glossary

Prigozhin, Yevgeny. (20.12 and elsewhere) Leader of the Wagner Group of mercenaries who assisted Russia early in the war with Ukraine. The group briefly turned against Putin and actually began to march toward Moscow, but abandoned the venture for reasons as yet unknown (or at least unpublished.) Prigozhin went briefly into exile but soon returned and rejoined the fight against Ukraine, only to be killed in an ostensibly accidental plane crash soon thereafter. See also **Siegfried**, below.

Punic (Languages). Augustine uses the word "Punic," which properly speaking would refer only to Carthage, to refer to anything African and non-Roman. Thus he uses "Punic languages" to indicate, effectively, anything but Latin and Greek. The "native" languages of Northern Africa at the time would have been early forms of the Berber family (i.e. Amazigh or Tamazight). Augustine's own language would have been Berber had not his parents, ambitious for the child to rise in the Roman hierarchy, enforced a strict Latin-only policy in the household and in his education. Arabic became the *lingua franca* of North Africa only after the Muslim conquests of the 7th and 8th centuries.

Punic Wars. The series of wars fought between the Roman Republic and Ancient Carthage, between 264 and 146 BCE. The first, which lasted 23 years, was called "the longest and most severely contested war in history" by historians of the era. The second was initiated by Hannibal's crossing of the Alps. For the third the Romans brought the fight to Carthage itself, in present day Tunisia, and sacked it.

Quirinus. When Romulus, legendary founder of Rome, was deified, his cult was assimilated into the cult of Quirinus, originally a Sabine deity.

Radagaisus. (d. 406). The Gothic king who led an invasion of Roman Italy in 405 with a plan to sacrifice the Roman Senators to the gods and to burn Rome to the ground. He did not succeed. He was executed and his fighters sold into slavery, so many of them that the slave market briefly collapsed, an anecdote Augustine (in 5.23) utilizes as a lesson in economics.

Rebus. A textual representation that combines words, individual letters and images to create a sentence. For example, one might say "To be or not to be" by using the numeral 2 with

glossary

pictures of a bee and picture of a knot for "not." Lacan held that dreams should be read like a rebus.

Rhinocorura. Mentioned by Augustine simply as a geographic reference in 16.24, Rhinocorura is described by the historian Strabo as a settlement of Ethiopians who had attempted to invade Egypt and were subsequently punished by having their noses cut off (the name means "severed noses" in Greek.) The story may conflate with one of an Egyptian border fortress called Tjaru, location unknown, which was purported to imprison officials who had committed crimes for which their noses had been cut off.

Rhodes. Stewart Rhodes (8.10), leader of the Oath Keepers, who attended the 1/6/21 inauguration heavily armed and prepared to reinstate Trump by force, was arrested for "seditious conspiracy" almost exactly one year later. He was convicted of seditious conspiracy and evidence tampering and sentenced to 18 years in prison. Trump pardoned him (along with dozens of other rioters) immediately upon taking office for his second term, in 2025.

Sabines. According to Livy, soon after the founding of Rome, Romulus became concerned that its population was almost entirely male and set about looking for wives for them, that they might increase. The Romans negotiated with the nearby Sabines to arrange marriages, but the Sabines were not enthusiastic, so the Romans took 30 of them by force, the famous "Rape of the Sabine Women."

Saguntines. In 219 BCE, the Iberian city of Saguntum, on the Mediterranean coast of present-day Spain, was a large and commercially prosperous town, allied with Rome, though Carthage was a vital trading partner. Hannibal's first assault against the empire, which triggered the Second Punic War (q.v.), was his siege of Saguntum. After stiff resistance over the course of eight months, Saguntum fell. Augustine cites the Saguntines, in 22.06, to refute Cicero's argument that no war should be undertaken except to preserve either "safety or honor." "For manifestly, if the Saguntines chose safety, they must break faith [i.e. with Rome]; if they kept faith, they must reject safety…"

Saint Augustine Marching 100. The marching band of St. Augustine High School in New Orleans, an historically black high school, known to locals as "the marching 100," is one

glossary

of the most popular attractions of the annual Mardi Gras parades.

Sallust. Gaius Sallustius Crispus, usually anglicized as Sallust (86 – c. 35 BCE), historian and politician, is the earliest known Latin-language Roman historian with surviving works to his name.

Samnite wars. The First, Second, and Third Samnite Wars (343–341 BCE, 326–304 BCE, and 298–290 BCE) were fought between the Roman Republic and the Samnites, who lived on a stretch of the Apennine Mountains south of Rome.

Sarah. Originally Sarai, wife of Abram (see Genesis 17-20) and also his half-sister. Early in their marriage Sarai appeared barren (despite the angels' promise that she and Abraham would spawn a great nation), and loaned Abraham her handmaid, Hagar, to bear him a child, which she did, and named him Ishmael. Soon after that, Sarah miraculously regained her fertility, got pregnant (in her 70s), and gave birth to Isaac. She then decided that Ishmael should not dilute Isaac's inheritance, and bade Abraham send Hagar and Ishmael away. Augustine utilizes this myth (in 15.02 and elsewhere) to describe certain characteristics of the two cities, with Sarah representing the City of God and Hagar, "the bond woman," the City of Man. When the three angels came to Mamre (q.v.) to announce to Abram that his wife would now, even at their advanced age, bear children, Abram and Sarai's names were changed to Abraham and Sarah.

Scipio. Publius Cornelius Scipio Nasica Corculum (c. 206–141 BCE) one of the most important Roman statesmen of the second century, advancing from consul to censor to *pontifex maximus* (chief priest) in 150 BCE, and finally *princeps senatus* (leader of the Senate, VP) in 147.

Scopes Trial. The State of Tennessee v. John Thomas Scopes, commonly referred to as the Scopes Monkey Trial, American legal case from 1925, popularized in media by the film *Inherit the Wind,* in which a high school teacher, John T. Scopes, was accused of violating Tennessee's Butler Act, which had made it unlawful to teach human evolution in any state-funded school. It is doubtful that Scopes ever actually taught evolution, but he incriminated himself deliberately merely to press the court decision. Scopes attorney, Clarence Darrow, utilized a logic based on the difficulty of measuring time before the sun

glossary

was created to argue that Darwinian evolutionary theory did not necessarily contradict the creation myth of Genesis. The argument bears striking similarity to Augustine's in 11.07.

Scorpion Squad. In February 2023 Tyre Nichols was beaten to death in Memphis by members of a "specialized police unit" called the Scorpion Squad. Five officers were charged with murder in the seemingly unprovoked beating, which one witness called "using him for a piñata."

Septuagint Scandal. The Greek Old Testament, or Septuagint ("the 70") is the earliest extant Koine Greek translation of books of the Hebrew Bible. The "scandal" was that the first Latin translations were actually taken from this Greek version rather than the original Hebrew. Augustine shows great concern, in several contexts, with the issue of translation. See 15.10 and 15.11. See also "Enoch," above.

Siegfried, Death of Siegfried. (20.12) The reference here is to Richard Wagner's Ring Trilogy, specifically the third opera, which is entitled *Siegfried*. Yevgeny Prigozhin (q.v. above) is supposed to have named his mercenary group "Wagner" in homage to this work. Prigozhin's fate (betrayal, we can surmise) appears to mirror Siegfried's, hence the conceit. The "horn call" in 20.12 is a reference to Siegfried's *leitmotif* in the opera.

Solon. (c. 630–560 BCE) Athenian statesman and lawmaker, remembered for his efforts to legislate against moral decline in archaic Athens. His legal writing was extremely influential in Athenian and, later, Roman law. He was also a prolific poet, often defending his political reforms in verse.

θεότης. theótis, deity, godhead, god-ness.

"tooth the size of my hand" (3.10, 15.09). Augustine professes here and elsewhere his belief in an historic age of giants, proven by his examination of a fossilized dinosaur tooth in his youth on a visit to Utica, recounted in 15.09, along with citations from Virgil, Pliny, and Homer.

Treaty of Tordesillas. The agreement signed by Spain and Portugal in 1494 dividing the new world, specifically South America, between them. Still sometimes cited in land disputes between indigenous and colonial folk in the Americas, the treaty is also famous for its cartographic inaccuracy, for while the intention was to divide South America equally between the two colonizers, the longitudinal line struck effectively gave everything except Brazil to Spain.

Tully. Affectionate nickname used by 19th century English translators to refer to Marcus Tullius Cicero (i.e. Cicero). Augustine refers to him as Tullius in 6.02 and several other places, but Dods translates "Tully" in only this instance.

Utica. Ancient Phoenician port in Tunisia near Hippo. (See "tooth…" above.)

about the author

Bill Lavender grew up in Arkansas—in Fayetteville, fortunately. In his twenties he came to New Orleans because he had met some poets from there and had read Bertolt Brecht's *Mahagonny*. Never planning to stay forever, always, in fact, on the verge of moving on, he is still there fifty years later.

He worked as a carpenter and contractor for many years before serving a 15-year sentence in academia, after which he returned to the business, without regret.

He started a small press in 1995 which has since grown to be Lavender Ink / Diálogos (lavenderink.org), and in 2011 he cofounded the New Orleans Poetry Festival.

He lives in New Orleans with his wife and partner of 30 years, Nancy Dixon.

Books by Bill Lavender

My ID, BlazeVOX, 2020

Three Letters (Novellas: Q; Little A; The Private I.) Spuyten Duyvil, 2020

surrealismo, Yauguru (Montevideo, Uruguay), 2018

La Police, Locofo Chaps, 2017

surrealism, Lavender Ink, 2016

Q, Trembling Pillow, 2013

Memory Wing, Black Widow, 2011

A Field Guide to Trees, Foothills Publishing 2011

Transfixion, Trembling Pillow, 2009

I of the Storm, Trembling Pillow, 2007

While Sleeping, Chax, 2004

look the universe is dreaming, Potes and Poets, 2003

Pentacl, Fell Swoop, 2001

Guest Chain, Lavender Ink, 1999

MadHat Press
MadHat Incorporated
PO Box 422, Cheshire, MA 01225
www.madhat-press.com

www.ingramcontent.com/pod-product-compliance
Lightning Source LLC
Chambersburg PA
CBHW031313160426
43196CB00007B/514